Explorations

Other books by the same author:

Revelation: The Birth of a New Age
Festivals in the New Age
The Laws of Manifestation
New Age Rhythms
Links with Space
Anthology: Vision of Findhorn
Towards a Planetary Vision
Reflections on the Christ
Relationship and Identity

These books and others of esoteric and social interest are available from Findhorn Publications. Please write for a free catalogue to Findhorn Publications, The Park, Forres IV36 OTZ, Scotland.

Explorations
Emerging aspects of the new culture

DAVID SPANGLER

FINDHORN PUBLICATIONS LECTURE SERIES

ISBN 0 905249 41 0

Cover design by Michael van der Ley (from an idea by Bob Knox)

Set in 11/12 point Journal Roman by Findhorn Publications

Printed and bound by Princo, Culemborg, Holland

Published by Findhorn Publications, The Park, Forres IV 36 OTZ, Scotland

MOST OF the following material represents information shared by David Spangler with the Findhorn Community during the years of 1970–1973. As such, it represents a stage in the growth of consciousness of both the community and of David. It was given in response to specific needs or questions existing within Findhorn during those years, and it was intended to be a foundation for further exploration and understanding. In no fashion does it represent a final statement on any of the principles mentioned. It is a particular reflection in time and space of the Universal, within which specific words, phrases and teachings must give way to the experience of the truth of Being and Reality. If this material assists you as such a guide, then it fulfils its purpose; it will have taken you beyond itself. If not, then perhaps it may still serve as an indication of where your guide may be by providing you with an experience of where it is not.

Findhorn Publications.

CONTENTS

Chapter

Chapter One
NEW AGE ENERGIES AND
THE SEED ATOM CONCEPT

IT IS A very ancient occult truth that everything in creation is alive; yet so accustomed do we become to life as we know it that this truth is misplaced on the shelf of our consciousness. Let us take it out and dust it off and see what relationship it has to our personal and collective future in the manifestation of those energies we associate with the new age.

The universe is made up of various energy manifestations which group themselves into dimensions. We live in a dimension we call the physical dimension because all of the energies to which we are most accustomed seem to manifest themselves in a fashion tangible to our five senses — they tend to have an aspect of solidity. There are other dimensions as well: etheric, astral, mental and spiritual. Because we are asked to unite in consciousness and work in co-operation with beings who do not apparently share physical life with us, it is important that we have a clear concept of what is involved in these various dimensions and the relationships between them.

These relationships can be described using the imagery of the piano in which the notes exist in a certain harmonic relationship expressed as octaves: both middle-C and the C above it, the first harmonic, which we will call high-C, express the same not in quality, but they express it at different frequencies and hence in a different dimension. In the same way, all that we see manifested on this level is duplicated in some corresponding form on all higher levels; and of course, the reverse is true, that is, all that exists on higher levels is duplicated on this one in some form or other.

The energy of higher levels, for example of the etheric or spiritual planes, cannot directly enter this realm for the same reason that, if you wish to hear what high-C sounds like, you cannot experience it by hitting middle-C on the piano. The frequencies are different. It is impossible for the frequency vibrations of higher levels to manifest in their natural state on any other dimension, simply by definition — for as soon as they manifest on a different

1

dimension they have changed their frequency.

When we talk about anchoring energies or bringing them down into manifestation, the picture one gets is something like grabbing hold of a rope trailing from a helium-filled balloon and tugging on it very hard in the hope that it will come to earth, or perhaps like finding within oneself or the environment some psychic socket into which one can plug an electrical cord and hope that the energy will flow. This is the concept of being a *channel* for higher energies, a concept whose inaccuracy will become more obvious. Just as with a ship on the ocean, where a mistake in navigation of only a small degree could result in the ship's ending up hundreds of miles from its destination if it has travelled over a sufficiently long course, so as we move into the new age an inaccuracy in our conceptualisation of what is happening to us can take us increasingly farther away from the very manifestation which we are seeking. A channel suggests something equivalent to a pipeline or a river bed or some device through which something else can flow. This may be a convenient image, but it expresses what is happening in too mechanical a way. We miss the sense of life and the sense of presence and the sense of cooperation that is so intimately a part of any activity between dimensions. The image that is formed is like some great cosmic current, perhaps the granddaddy of electricity, descending onto the soil, the trees and the people of places like Findhorn. We are bathed in it as if someone in the higher planes had turned on a spotlight and there we are, revealed.

Some people find this image very comfortable because it makes it appear that the thing is happening without their having to co-operate with it. They can either bathe in it or they can move out of it. However, now that very beautiful and significant energies are attempting to manifest in the world, it is important that we alter this concept.

What we are really dealing with is life. All energy, no matter what its form of manifestation, is alive. More than that, it has intelligence. It is a being. It may not be a being such as we are familiar with, such as you or I, but that is because a human individual is actually a synthesis of many energies. We are a combined form and we have certain abilities because of this, which other beings, more specialised spiritual beings, do not possess. These energies are all living presences nonetheless, and within the limits of human conceptualisation they can externalise themselves

2

and speak to us. In fact, when we speak with the nature world—the devas and the elementals—we are communicating with what in essence are energy forms, alive and intelligent.

For the purposes of describing this, let us examine one individual who is seeking to become a point of focus for energy. According to the old concepts a person would simply open oneself up through various means of preparation and the energy would flow through. We would say it is necessary for one to step aside, to remove one's personality and allow the energies to flow purely through one's being. What we are actually witnessing, however, is a different phenomenon altogether: that of an individual who has been able to reproduce in oneself a *lower octave equivalent* of those energies, so that one is manifesting on the lower planes a duplicate of what they represent on the higher planes. Through the law of resonance, the equivalent energies (like middle-C and high-C) become one and the oneness is made manifest.

Some people are trained to do this. They have had their training in other lives, so it comes to them very easily, and those of us who observe this in them may miss the actual mechanics of what is occurring. When we attempt to duplicate it in our own lives, we find that it is difficult and we become depleted. We find that we become irritated or distressed in other ways.

The best way to describe this process is to use the terms of marriage. There is the meeting, the courtship, the marriage and the consummation, and then the birth of the child. I find these images helpful, because they suggest a sense of life and of blending with another presence, another living being. Now, people's true nature is found in the auric field. Human beings are energy beings, but they are also a combination of energies all blended together. They have the capacity, as if some keyboard, to strike any number of harmonies and notes, so that they possess within them the equivalent of all possible energies that can come from higher levels.

There may be energies coming from these higher levels that are completely new to us, and hence we have to learn to sense new harmonies. We have to learn to sense new patterns of putting the notes together. We have within us, because of the combination of energies that we have built up through the ages of our evolution and experience, the ability to produce the equivalent of higher-plane energies that may never have been known on this planet before. We say, "How can we be attuned to these new energies when they are so totally new?" We can be attuned because within us exists the exact counterpart on the lower realms. The example of music describes this well. The first time that we hear a given piece of modern music, it may seem so totally unrelated to the concepts we have formed of harmony, tone, music and form that it is difficult to relate to it at all, and we experience distress. However, when we hear it again, since we have heard it once before the links have been formed. The second time we hear it we may not like it any better but we will recognise it with a greater degree of awareness. It will not seem so strange. Gradually, if we hear it often enough, we suddenly find that we are perceiving within that music new forms of harmony, new forms of structure, that are totally different from anything we have experienced before, yet they elicit a response of understanding.

Likewise when energies pour upon us from higher levels and make themselves manifest, through someone's voicing them through a teaching or performing them through an action, they may at first glance appear very strange, almost non-understandable. Because we contain within us the ability to respond to any conceivable energy coming to this planet, however, there is a response that grows within us. It may be quite small at first, but it is there. I call this the 'meeting'.

Some of you have had this experience in personal life. Perhaps the first time you met the person to whom you are married or with whom you are in love you did not like them or felt nothing. But as you got to know them you suddenly discovered that chords were struck in your being that were very important to you, and this developed into what we call 'love', a desire to blend together. First, however, there was the meeting.

When we contact these energies we are actually coming into the presence of living beings. It is perhaps personalising it too much to say that they have feeling, but in a sense they do have sensitive awareness and they are bound to obey the laws of resonance or the law of sympathy—like attracts like. These beings cannot approach any point, dimension, or person in which there is not a sympathetic response. The person cannot just say to these beings "I love you—come on in", because it does not work that way. The aura of the individual has to begin to resonate like a tuning fork in harmony with the energies that these beings represent. The only way it can do that is for us to find within ourselves an equivalent harmony.

I will use two examples here. If I want to love universally, I encounter the concept of 'universal love'. Yet I do not know how to go about it—perhaps in reality I cannot stand people in the mass. I may be at a loss to know how to express that higher octave. I do not have to struggle or strain, however. All I need to begin is to find the equivalent pattern on a lower level and resonate to that. The lowest level in human experience may be the sexual level. The next level would be simply personal love, singling out an individual and learning to love that person on all levels, to get the love vibration resonating within the being. Then it is possible to establish a relationship with that greater being whom we call the Christ who is the embodiment of universal love. The key is not to stop or become caught on any lesser level but to use it to discover the essential quality or resonance that can expand into the next level.

The second example occurs in Jesus' case. We say that Jesus was the channel for the cosmic Christ, and yet this is an inaccuracy. Before Jesus could manifest the cosmic octaves of Christhood he had to achieve his personal Christhood; he had to resonate within himself to the Christ consciousness, and it was this resonance that created the harmony between these two octaves. If I strike middle-C and the string of the high-C is not damped, it will vibrate as well, though I may have to be sensitive in my hearing to perceive it. If I strike the chord of Christhood in my personal life, the cosmic Christ will resonate equally. The cosmic Christ could not enter the Earth plane without a point of resonance. This is really the significance of what Jesus did: he sounded the Christ note and as a consequence he built up in his aura a resonating field that was identical with—though of a lower octave than—the field of the cosmic Christ. That being was able then to unite with the auric field of Jesus, and the product of that union was, in essence, a son, a child, a manifestation of blended energy which is what we have called The Christ.

Next there is a period of 'courtship', and this is very important. It may be a very swift period or it may be a lengthy one, but it is that period in which we come to terms with what these energies represent. It may be through learning to understand "What *does* Findhorn mean?"; "What *do* the teachings mean?"; "What *does* the new age mean?" As we meditate upon this within ourselves

5

we come to understand, to resonate within those concepts in our aura, and this allows these being-presences to come closer to us until eventually they can merge completely with our auric field. We are sounding their note in exact harmony, though on a lower octave.

When that happens, a mystical 'marriage' occurs. The being literally is empowered to enter our auric field, or our auric field is able to blend with its, and out of those combined energies can be produced a directive wave of broadcasting energy—a manifestation which is the 'child' of that relationship. When we think of these beings or this energy as a mechanical action and of ourselves as channels of it, we do not tend to make the necessary efforts to blend truly.

This is very important. These beings cannot enter this dimension without our assistance. That is what we are here for—that is why we have taken physical embodiment. That is why the splendour and infinite complexity of our human souls, developed through ages of experience, has taken on flesh: so that these beings would have points of compatability, individuals that could resonate and do the work on this level which would enable them to enter or set up the resonating field through which the child could be born and made manifest. It is a creative partnership that exists between us and these regents, the various beings who represent the energies of God. We may call them devas, or the Lords of the Seven Rays—it does not matter as long as we realise we are involved in a living situation, not a mechanical one. There is a certain lack of responsibility in just stepping aside and letting these beings function through us, because we have evolved on this level a sensitivity which these beings do not possess. We have come here to learn what it means to become involved in matter. This gives us a sensitivity to matter, form and density, which these higher beings who have never experienced them do not possess but which they can manifest by sharing our experience when we blend with them. It is just like any marriage: the partners share the experience of their lives up to the point when they came together. This enriches their unity and it enables them to do things together that they could not do when they were separate. This is why our personalities are very important—they represent the links we have formed with the physical plane.

We should look upon our personalities as being a creative tool.

The tool may have some rough edges, some links that are not useful, and this is why we seek to work with our personalities. Since we aim to free our consciousness to appreciate all the life of the universe, and because the personality is a tool fashioned from Earth and linked to Earth, it is naturally going to take the point of view that only the things of the physical level are important. It is a tricky balance. We cannot absolutely destroy that point of view, because then we destroy our links with the physical plane and are useless for the purposes of creativity on this level, though we may have happy, jolly experiences in floating around on higher levels. On the other hand, we must in consciousness go beyond the links of the personality if we are to use them, for otherwise they use us and we are limited to their point of view.

Some people are more closely linked to the personality than others: some have a small keyboard to play on and others have a wider one. The people with the wider keyboards and the lesser links, or the freer links, have the opportunity to become what is known occultly as a 'seed atom'.

This is a very simple concept—it means the point around which manifestation can occur. A seed atom as an individual is simply one who catches a vision that no one else has caught and is able to do something about it. For example: we are all in the community centre just sitting around and chatting, and one of us thinks, "Wouldn't it be fun if we had some singing? Let's get up to the piano and play and have some community singing." If that person just has the idea and doesn't do anything with it then the idea is lost—it remains on an abstract level. If the person gets up and talks to other people and says, "Wouldn't it be nice if one of us got up and played the piano and we had some singing?" other people are likely to say, "Yes, that would be nice—who will do it? Oh well, someone will do it" and the energy gets dispersed as everyone wonders who is going to play. But if the person gets up, moves to the piano and begins to play, he then provides a focus, a centre of attraction. All those people who like to sing or like to listen suddenly think, "Music!" They are attracted to its opportunity.

The person playing at the piano is a seed atom. He has become a point around which the manifestation of community singing can organise itself. Those people that do not like community singing, maybe because all the people who are singing have horrible voices, can leave. But that is a form of organisation as well, because at least things are not moving in chaos. They have now become separated into those who stay and those who leave. The entire action has in essence crystallised around this one individual who caught the vision, got up and did something about it. The vision became alive in that person's aura and reproduced itself physically through the piano.

Now, let us imagine that the person has been playing for five hours and has become very weary; but for some reason, possibly because no one intends to work the next day, everyone decides to sing the whole night through. The person who has established himself as the piano player has set the thing into motion. He can then relinquish his position as seed atom. It is no longer necessary for him to be that point of focus because now other people have caught the idea, and as soon as he gets up from the piano someone else can sit down and take over. The idea has gathered its own momentum and will continue to propagate itself in manifestation.

It is the same thing in the life of those great beings we have been discussing. With them, seed individuals become a point through which these beings can manifest. It is necessary for such individuals to do something about it: they cannot just sit in meditation and think how lovely it is to walk hand in hand with these great beings, because the great beings will not put up with it. The actual energy of resonance has to be set into its full power through action of some form. For some kinds of energy this could be mental action like writing, discussing, or visiting. For other kinds of energy it has to be physical action: digging cesspits, digging roads, weeding gardens, doing something physically. As the individuals do something physically, they are in essence embodying the vision. They are playing, as it were, the lower octave counterpart, and that enables their auras to resonate in harmony with these beings—to have the power of these spiritual beings added to the individuals' own and manifested through their action, their discussion, their writing and whatever they have been guided to. The child is born.

Once one person starts doing it, other people become attracted. That is what a seed atom is for. By the law of sympathy, like attracting like, other people who have the same vague vision suddenly see it crystallise before them. They are attracted to it and come and begin to work with the seed individual. As they catch the vision, the power of the greater being spreads out into their auras—now it is a group marriage. The greater being is a polygamist—it is married to a number of individuals. As time goes along each of these other individuals in turn can become a seed atom.

These higher beings are not simple beings—their own nature is highly complex. For example, the Christ has many manifestations—Universal Love has many manifestations. It is not all sweet and kind. It can be hard and demanding at times. Other people may be able to play counterpoint and add other harmonies that the original seed atom was not aware of because of his need to focus and get the original thing going; but as they are encouraged and become able to supply their unique action, their form of childbirth—the energy, the life of this greater being—is able to spread out and be released further, and so it grows. Instead of being a seed atom it becomes a seed molecule—more people are attracted and the power propagates itself.

That is what happened at Findhorn. Initially Peter and Eileen and Dorothy represented the seed atom; then Joanie and others came. They acted in faith to externalise something—even though they may have had only one caravan at the time, they acted as if they had a number of caravans and a community already existed. The vision was able to resonate within them. The being, a small aspect of the being who represents the energies at Findhorn, was able to come into closer union with them and effect marriage. As this developed, other beings—the nature spirits and so forth—were able to enter and become part of the action. Eventually more people were attracted until a community was formed.

It is important to realise that every member of this community is another seed atom. You each can form a mystical marriage with the energies, the beings, the life that is here at Findhorn, and produce your own contribution to the community. It is necessary that this be done because that is the way the energies can unfold and the life spread. That is what a community means.

It is very important what is happening at Findhorn, for it is a break from the whole idea of government in human society which is based on authority operating downward. This is true even in a democracy—everyone elects a president and then sits back and lets the president tell them what to do. Eventually they no longer have a democracy. This has been the pattern of human life, but now in the new age we seek to break this and to realise a different one, a pattern of uniting with a living universe and realising that that universe through its own life externalises its own government. The being who is the collective overseer of Findhorn is actually the governing source. As a seed atom for it the members of the core group exercise a certain amount of authority, and in an occult sense this is proper. You, however, must break the pattern of reliance on an outside point of authority and realise that unfoldment from within. Then to an increasing degree the authority of the vision and the ensouling life become manifest.

The greatest help to the seed atom is for other people to begin to resonate in harmony—not with the person but with that with which the person is resonating in harmony. Generally that means the same thing, but not always, because each one is unique and has a unique contribution. Jesus required twelve disciples to become the resonators of the Christ pattern—to allow it to enter more fully than it could do through him as a single individual. All of you who are part of Findhorn, those of you who have committed your lives to the vision of Findhorn, must seek to unfold your own part of that vision.

The only way that Findhorn will survive is as a growing organism. In an organism everything shares its life, not in sacrifice to the whole but in contribution to the whole. Thereby the life of the organism is enhanced. This is an occult law of manifestation, and it is the way energies are anchored and released. One person cannot anchor an energy. It takes a number of people who, through the resonance of their lives, by being love, being light, being harmony, can broadcast that energy to the environment. Then others begin to resonate with it—it is the principle of the tuning fork. Not every note expresses the same thing but all notes are required; from one person playing on the keyboard of that person's consciousness,we suddenly have a whole orchestra of people creating a triumphant symphony.

This is challenging work because we need to work with our personalities—our links with Earth. The personality is simply nothing more than the way we respond to things. If I say I have a negative personality, all that that means is that I respond to life negatively—those are my links. To change them I need to respond positively, in whatever way I understand that. The personality is not a static condition. We tend to think of it as *being* something, but it is not: it is a state of continually changing relationships. While we need to maintain those links, for that is what the higher beings require, we must strive to see beyond them with as high or clear a vision as possible.

We have a great future ahead of us as human beings moving into the new age. There are aspects of ourselves that have not been revealed to us, aspects that are closely linked to the nature world, for example, which require us to do more than just cooperate with the nature kingdom and allow it to become one with us. Once the patterns within us that have been held in secret for centuries are revealed, we will become more truly human. We do have the capacity to synthesise energies. Where the forces of nature may play single harmonies, people have the capacity to play symphonies. As we learn to see the universe as a living entitiy with which we merge in a sense of love and cooperation, and as we maintain the resultant marriage, so will we be exalted. So will we truly manifest ourselves as gods of Earth and disciples of God moving out into a living universe.

Chapter Two
EDUCATION IN THE NEW AGE

'EDUCATION In The New Age'—the title implies a great deal, but our subject has little to do with specific kinds of education.

Instead, we shall examine what a human being is. Education is not an end in itself; it is a process that people have evolved in order to help them become more creative, better informed, better adapted to the needs of world and society, and more capable. In many ways, though, education seems now to do everything except make a better human being. With its growth as an institution, education has become a vested interest within society and is often looked upon as an end in itself. Everything that people have created, however—all their institutions, schools, governments, churches—are designed not for the organisation's benefit, but to do something for human beings. The institutions are, in theory, service organisations; as soon as they cease to give the proper kind of service, they have forfeited their right to existence and should be replaced by something which can meet the changing needs of the human race which they were created to serve in the first place.

In order to gain a vision of what education will encompass in the new age—in an age of humanity's rapidly expanding consciousness—we want to take a look at people and see what these beings are whom these institutions are designed to serve. We will gain insight from this into some specific directions for those of us who are, or are becoming, teachers.

Since the new age implies a break from materialistic thought, I feel quite free to speak of the inner and esoteric aspects of humanity and of its institutions. In common with all life, humanity shares what has variously been called divinity, the Christ within, the God-spark, the Godhead, oneness with the Creator and so on. It possesses an essentially indefinable quality of being which is highly resistant to being categorised, labelled, shelved, dissected, placed into a laboratory and studied. It can be denied but it cannot be lost, and it will persistently manifest itself in one form or another. Everything in creation possesses this quality, and in this manner everything is equal. In the sense of growth, of helping a person to become more capable, better informed and more skilful, the word 'education' has very little meaning. We do not know what growth means in God's terms, because to us God symbolises and manifests all that is perfect and unchanging. We are coming to realise, however, that though God may manifest as perfection to us, it is also a manifestation of dynamics and motion. We call this motion 'life', the expression of God throughout creation.

There has been some question posed as to the relationship between the various hierarchies, the various levels of cosmic and planetary authority, and God. Where do these fit in? How do they relate to each other? There is a perfect example of that at Findhorn. We can look upon God as being a highly potent seed, one which requires cultivation by skilled gardeners, and some gardeners are more skilled than others. All of creation is the tending of the development and expression of this indefinable light and presence. We do not need to know *why* this is so; it is enough that we see that it is so and experience its manifestation in our life.

The entire universe, all of creation as we know it, is an educational process in that everything around us represents a drawing-out from within of some inner potential as yet unexpressed and a giving to it of the ability to express.

When we speak about the evolution of humanity, the evolution of nature, or the evolution of the planet, we are talking about the transformation of form. Each new form becomes more able to express the potential inherent in the previous form. For example, the sapling is able to express the potential inherent in the seed; and the tree is able to express more fully, and to make real, the potential inherent in the sapling, and so on to the production of new seed and new trees. Everything about us is involved in this educational process. It is almost as if the universe is divided into that which is being called forth, and that which has already been called forth and is in turn calling forth that which is behind it, or beneath it, or awaiting.

As I unfold further, it becomes an inescapable aspect of life that I must in turn call something else forth in some way, whether verbally or through living example and action. My life is part of an educational process, a calling forth from others who may not be expressing what I am, that ability to express it. 'It' can be anything. If I am a painter, I call forth to the seed of painting in other

13

people. Some will respond and some will not. Even if I do not set about to do it, the mere fact of sitting on the beach and painting a seascape may inspire a passerby with the thought that "I'd like to do that myself. Maybe I should investigate this."

Whatever we are, wherever we are, whatever we are doing, we are part of a complete educational process. All of life is an educational process. One of the first changes in the new age—one which we can see happening right now around us—is that education will cease to be related to a specific time of life or to a specific kind of experience, such as sitting in a classroom for five hours a day and being the receptor of information or skills. We will see instead that everything we partake in is education in some form or another.

Individuals who realise that everything around them is teaching them, and that they in turn are teaching everything around them, become much more open in their consciousness. That is really what the new age is all about: an openness, a freedom to move and to receive, to give and to be, and not to remain encased in a static form. I worked for two years in adult education and I met many interesting people. Most of them were retired, and they had this tremendous sense of, "Well, just because I'm over fourty, or fifty, or sixty, why should that stop me from continuing to learn?" I had one woman in my class who was eighty-five, and she was busy working on a college degree. Why should she be limited to saying, "Well, I may only live for another year, so why bother?" She had a sense of life being a continual expansion in which the moment you stop expanding you stop living.

The first thing that is happening, then, is this expansion of the word 'education' from a purely institutional and formal definition into one which encompasses all of life's experiences and potentials. Within that, we see something else happening. At the present time, as a culture, we are extremely outward oriented. Education has come to mean something entirely different from its original meaning. The word stems from a root which means 'to lead out', not 'to put in', but education has come to mean 'putting in'. In my experience, teachers have had the idea that the people who are sitting in front of them are vessels ready to receive what the teacher has to offer. Our whole life is oriented that way, so it is not the teacher's fault if that is the way they are going to approach their class. If this is the teacher's approach, the class can hardly help but enter into it, and it implies a certain materialism. I mean 'materialism' in the sense of looking upon a person as a material object

14

rather than as a living organism, looking upon a person almost like a cup to be filled—a rather impersonal, objective view.

Because our whole society tends to be based on this, we look for everything to come to us from outside: happiness, love, fulfilment, information, peace. We are in a constant state of searching and seeking, running hither and thither. It is only logical that we look for education as coming from outside and see it in its informational context: for we learn so many mathematical theorems, so many laws of chemistry; we memorise all these dates from history; we experience a constant pouring into the being of external information.

Much of this information is obviously of value and is highly useful. Those who have only recently emerged from the educational mill, however, realise how easy it is to form a frame of mind that is perfect at soaking up information and giving it back in a parrot-like form, to get a grade but later discovering that none of it has sunk in. Why should it, when the being, itself, is not a vessel to have things poured into it?

Even though we have talked about the body's being a vehicle of the spirit, this is not an accurate description, and we do need to start being accurate. This is the time for changing some old concepts. The body is not the vehicle of anything. The body is actually the projection of a central core. It is not an automobile that a soul is running around in and driving; it is an actual projection outward from something that is within. The body itself is a manifestation of an educative process occurring on etheric levels; the soul, the environment, the parents, all these have conspired to lead out, from within, a physical manifestation. As soon as this concept of the projected nature of the body becomes real to us, we gradually discover, maybe quickly discover, that we have absolute control over the body because we can change the projection.

Here a new concept emerges. It is a concept suggested by *Limitless Love and Truth* in various revelations of the past when the author uses the term 'nuclear evolution'. That term may mean many things; like so many images that come from 'upstairs', it does not have a single meaning. One of its meanings is that the nucleus, whether we are discussing it in biological, physical, or chemical terms, always represents the centre of control, the centre from which control and life springs. It is the core point. Nuclear evolution suggests a picture of evolution proceeding outward from

15

a centre—which ties it in with the concept of education, which is a leading outward from what is within.

If we can grasp this concept, the purpose of education becomes not only one of dispensing information, but also of becoming an evocative presence, a magnet, a stimulator to draw out of people what is already there. The teacher feels no exclusive responsibility to put things in. They feel a responsibility to provide an environment, which may be mental, emotional or physical, in which things can be drawn out, and can indeed spring forth joyously, gladly and automatically—not so much like pulling teeth, but drawing out into ecstasy, because life should be an ecstasy and education should be the revelation of that ecstasy.

At the present time what humanity has in the way of information is exploding at such a rate that in the next ten years it will double, and it will double again five years after that, and probably double again in two and one-half years thence, until we reach a point where every day all the information that humanity knows doubles itself. We are at a point now where it is possible to store information on molecular patterns within certain specially designed crystals. You can carry the whole Library of Congress around in a little crystal. The only problem is that there is not yet a way of getting the information back out; but it is possible to put it there.

Education will become, therefore, an exercise in training an individual to draw out the capacity to reach deeply into the underlying essences of life so as to by-pass this immense mass of detailed information, which is multiplying at such a fantastic rate, and see things in their wholeness rather than in their analysed pieces. If people need to see the analysed pieces, they can be given a means of gaining access to them. As an example, there is research being done in America today to provide private offices and clinics with instant access to computer memory-banks, containing all the information from the medical journals being published monthly— for there are hundreds of them coming out every month with new research, new information on symptoms and so on, that no doctor could keep up with and still see patients (if you are unable to see a doctor it may be because he is too busy reading the journals!). Thus, if a doctor has a patient, he has a little typewriter in his office onto which he types into the computer what the symptoms are, and the computer relays to him all the latest information he needs to know about its treatment.

The time when education is only a transmitter of information is rapidly passing, because there is too much information to transmit. The coming day belongs to evolving humanity, which is not an informational being, a file cabinet walking around on two legs, but a tremendously creative source which can draw in information if it is needed, and is able to see things in terms of wholeness rather than being swallowed up by little bits and pieces. Such a humanity can work with principles of synthesis. To help such a humanity evolve is surely one of the destined functions of education in the new age.

Another factor which relates to this is that modern educational techniques and approaches do not permit freedom—they create a state of mental and emotional regimentation. Esoterically, however, we realise that every individual is absolutely unique. People have no counterpart anywhere in creation. As a consequence they require a great deal of freedom to bring out that uniqueness. I cannot give you uniqueness—I cannot impose uniqueness upon you. If I tried, I might make you something unique, but it would actually be a reflection of my own uniqueness. You would become a mirror image, and most likely a distorted one, of myself.This is another reason why education must turn from a process acting from the outside upon the being, to a process inviting what is within the being to step out and make itself known. Uniqueness cannot be transmitted; it can only be invited and encouraged to express itself. This requires a great deal of freedom, and each individual requires this freedom.

Aligned with freedom is the need for discipline. The soul needs freedom, and the soul is free, but it is quite another thing to give the personality the same kind of freedom. The freedom that the indwelling presence within humanity can handle is something quite different from the freedom that the personality can handle. The two are complementary, but if the soul's freedom is going to express itself it requires the discipline of the personality.

This is very apparent in many fields. I will give you an analogy: imagine someone trying to run with leather soles on a sheet of ice, and you will have an idea of a soul attempting to manifest its creative power through an undisciplined personality. There is no friction. There is nothing that that soul can push against that is solid, nothing against which it can exert some force to move out into the world. Just like the ice-runner, there is nothing there to

17

give a solid footing, and so the personality keeps sliding and slipping and falling. Yet this discipline cannot be regimentation; it must simply be discipline.

We can see this in the following way. We are surrounded by a rich, sensual universe. It imposes upon us many kinds of impressions, many kinds of opportunities, and if we attempt to manifest all of them we end up manifesting nothing. The personality—the emotional, mental, and in some cases physical side of people—is a reactive mechanism. It is designed to react to outer stimuli. Without discipline it will always react to outer stimuli and the person has no freedom at all. The people who appear to be very free because they do anything they want, are the people who are most limited because, in fact, they are doing nothing that they want. It is the inner spirit that enables us to act, rather than simply to react to stimuli, but in order to act we need to listen to that spirit and not to the thousands and millions of voices that are screaming at us from our environment to do various things.

We do this in meditation. This is why we are asked to meditate. Meditation does not contain any great magical power, it is only an opportunity for us to experience stillness, to experience listening to only one voice at a time—the one that is within. Everybody knows how frustrating it can be to attempt to listen to a conversation or speak in a crowded room with everyone else talking. It takes a great deal of concentration to be able to do it, and some people cannot do it at all; they become very frustrated and disturbed if they have to talk to people over the din of other people's voices.

Discipline for the soul and for the personality simply means providing an atmosphere of constant inner peace, so that we are not simply mechanisms responding to an environment but are creative presences unfolding what lies within us. That is why discipline is vital to the educative process. If I insult you and you strike me, that is simply a reaction; I have not called anything forth from you, really. I have simply stimulated your mechanism to do something, like pulling a string; and all of us will remain puppets as long as life has this capacity to make us react on its own terms. Whenever little things happen to us, we respond in reaction to them rather than creating in the moment what we really want to be, or do, or say.

If that which lies within us is to come out, if we are to become educated and not just pumped full of information and physical

18

skills, then we are required to invite it out. It is not up to teachers to do this. Ultimately each of us must be our own educator; we must permit what is within us the freedom and the opportunity to spring out. Teachers can help us to do this, educators can help us to do this, but ultimately it is our own responsibility, and this is where discipline comes in. That is why we have it. Not everyone can be similarly disciplined because everyone is unique. I believe that the educative process of the new age will be staffed by individuals sensitive to the personality level—the emotional, mental and physical levels of the individual they are dealing with—so that each one can be disciplined in the way that is unique to that person's own pattern.

Again, discipline is not something to be imposed from without. It is something that must be inspired from within. Ultimately we must have self-discipline, not imposed discipline, and this comes through understanding of self. We may find that some form of outside discipline is useful to get us started, however. Originally, discipline meant learning. It was part of the concept of education, leading out so that we could hear what was within us and give it a chance to express, rather than simply to respond in the moment.

Education in the future will deliver to humanity the most priceless gift of all, which is absolute freedom. People have sought freedom for centuries. They have looked for it in political ways, in healing ways, in medical ways, in psychological ways and in religious ways. But a person is free only when educated; when constantly educating oneself and leading out from within oneself what is most deeply there, in perfect awareness of one's environment and its needs.

This last point brings in another aspect, for what lies within us is not only inside ourselves, but also within everything else as well. If I want to lead out what is inside of me *here*, I have to learn also the art of leading it out from what is out *there*, so that I break down the separation between my personality and your personality, my body and all the rest of the world, my being and the rest of creation. Ultimately, what I am leading out is that presence which is universally the presence within all creation.

In this way, I am not being educated in an isolated state. I am being educated, initially, to draw out from within myself my uniqueness so that I can subsequently blend that uniqueness with other people, and draw out from the potential of our united efforts patterns of consciousness, being, relationship and awareness, that all of us could not do singly and alone. In this way we become educators of the universe—which is our true function.

Everything is an educative process. It is emerging from within us, and in turn we have to help it out from everything else. In this way the God-presence continues to expand and unfold. Every day becomes a new age. Every moment becomes a new revelation, and there is no end to it.

Education in the new age is going to become the very process of life itself. It will become every action a being is involved with in its relationship with others, as it realises that through those relationships it is educating creation. It is leading out from within creation the potentials that have been there and making them real. At the same time, it is having led out from within itself its own potentials, and having them made real. There is always this constant growth, and for me the divinity of humanity is its ability to grow. As soon as humanity stops growing it has lost its divinity, for it is not expressing that divinity. Humanity becomes something else—a kingdom unto itself.

Because we are living in a material form world, and we need to know things about form in order to deal with it, I am sure that educational institutions will continue. They will be vastly modified, however, to fit in with a more expanded philosophy of humanity and its education. They will be decentralised. They will become clusters. Already we have the capacity to place in every home a computer link to the accumulated knowledge of humanity; and more than that, to place in every home the ability to experience things happening anywhere in the world, through television.

As humanity expands beyond these mechanical aspects and realises the incredible freedom of its soul, and as it gives that freedom a chance to unfold, then indeed the entire universe will be its home. Any information that people need will be forthcoming, because they will have learned what they are and what they can do with it rather than being dependent upon that information to build their being. In the future, other patterns will need to be considered, like the concept of reincarnation—after all, this is not the first time we have been educated here, in an esoteric sense. We have all gone through many patterns of learning and relearning; and if those memory veils could be partially lifted, if it is right to lift them, then undoubtedly that pattern may develop. That is a secondary consideration, however, because things we learned in the past may no longer be applicable. If I learned two thousand years ago that the earth was flat, and similar facts which were the most up-to-date scientific knowledge of the time, it really would not help me a great deal to remember it now.

There are patterns of creativity that are open to us through attunement to the other kingdoms of life, the angelic kingdoms: in the same way that the devas and elementals work with the building of plant form, there is a similar pattern, an analogous pattern, operating within the development of human form and consciousness, and this can be worked with. Such potentials are sure to unfold, but they are specifics; the general pattern is as I have stated it: that humanity is going to expand its concept of what education means, and will realise that education is the expression of God active in the universe and within people.

DISCUSSION

Q. Is it true that there cannot really be a separation between teachers and parents, because both are performing a similar function in the new age?

A. That is true, but there is more to be said on that subject. A parent is by definition one who gives life to a child, to a new being, and everything else becomes the child's teachers as well. It would assist in this process, however, if after the child has been born the parents forgot that they were parents and began thinking in terms of being teachers. Teachers have one advantage—they are not using the child as a vehicle for their own interests. Sometimes, of course, this happens, but it happens a great deal more often in families, which is natural: the child is there, it carries on the family traditions. The kind of education a child receives in the family often imposes on the child the group thought-form of the family itself. If the child is keyed into that thought-form, it will merge with it naturally. I think if parents could be more impersonal and yet loving at the same time, and think of themselves as teachers, they would then encourage the child to develop its uniqueness.

Q. I gather that in the new age wisdom will replace knowledge?

A. Here we run into a question of semantics—it depends on what we mean by the words. With that provision, I would say "yes". Wisdom is an odd creature. It is actually the happy marriage of what has come from outside with what is emerging from within—a blend of both. I cannot be wise if I am isolated, therefore, I require knowledge—knowledge being a communing with what is around me. If I have knowledge only, however, I become like a librarian. I have all this information stacked away but it hasn't become part of me.

Knowledge is really the touch of life upon us, prior to the full embrace. It makes us aware of what is there, but then we have to go deeper. It is when we have broken through knowledge into oneness that we have wisdom. Wisdom to me includes such things as love, intelligence, and awareness. Without love there can be no wisdom; wisdom is the manifestation of knowledge infused with the power of love.

Q. Within group life, should the education of children become the responsibility of everybody and not only a specialised group who are called teachers?

A. Yes. Here again is the principle that all life is educating itself, and everything we touch is an educative experience in one way or another; and in group life where children are free to move about, everyone they meet will in some way play an educative role. That is why we cannot just say: "Well, there's the school building up there, where the kids are and the learning takes place." That is not true; the learning takes place for all of us wherever we are in the moment.

Q. On the other hand, is discipline the responsibility of the parents?

A. Wherever the child is, wherever anyone is, one is involved in a learning experience. As far as discipline goes, it needs to be consistent, otherwise it becomes as chaotic as the sensory life that surrounds us. Discipline is not designed to make people obey, or to curb them. Discipline is designed to give people a sense of inner strength, so that they have something to push against in life. If people have a sense of discipline

22

they are like an artist; artists have to be disciplined before they can perform their art. This should never become conditioning, however, because the moment it does it destroys our creativity. Discipline should evolve from a point of telling the child, "Do this, don't do that," and "this is why," to a point of giving the child the chance to exercise that discipline through responsibility, so that it knows what is behind it and it becomes an inner part of that child. The people who should do this are the ones who are with the child most often—in most cases the parents. If everyone in a group attempts to discipline a child, it is going to get as many different kinds of discipline as there are group members, and that is chaotic.

One of the best ways of establishing discipline within a child is to give the child a sense of its own dignity, its own beauty and its own power. Most discipline, I have found, has the opposite effect; it destroys the child. It makes the child feel, "Now, I've done wrong, I'm sinful, I'm wrong; I am this, I am that." When discipline is used as a punishment it creates within the child a lack of a sense of dignity and creativity, and naturally it will rebel against that. The child should never fear discipline. The parent should ensure that the child realises it is not being punished or rewarded through discipline; it is being given tools to strengthen itself, and to allow what it is to emerge.

Chapter Three
HEALING: GOOD AND EVIL

ALTHOUGH the subject of this chapter is healing, we are going to explore a far wider realm than that. Healing is part of a greater whole which involves the orientation of consciousness itself, and leads us into such concepts as the reality (or non-reality) of good and evil, light and dark.

We dwell in a world of consciousness, and everything that exists in our physical realm reflects that consciousness. We dwell in worlds of energy, for consciousness is energy and all forms of energy are the expression of consciousness. Energy can be many things. It can be love. It can be qualities of feeling and thought. It can be physical energy. It can be energy which lights our lights and warms our homes. When I use the term 'energy', I am using it in a very broad sense: I mean by it the capacity to do work, the capacity to effect change and to create some kind of manifestation.

The universe in which we live is a manifestation of consciousness, but it is a highly creative and growing consciousness. There is no grand blueprint for the universe in terms of forms. There is, however, the unfoldment of that consciousness which is always in existence—we may call this the consciousness of God, if we wish. We may call it that only if we include ourselves within that concept, however, for there is no separation. On whatever level this master consciousness or universal consciousness seeks to work, it is always seeking to unfold from within itself new possibilities, new potentials, new realities. This is the essence of divinity: the ability to create and to grow, not to remain crystallised in a particular form.

In order to make this possible the universe is, roughly speaking from our point of view, divided into two kinds of basic manifestations: the one we call spirit and the other we call matter. They are essentially the same thing. Physically they are related through Einstein's very famous equation of $E=mc^2$. If we take that same equation and relate it in an analogous fashion to the higher realms, then all spirit and all matter are related through the 'equals sign' of consciousness.

Matter represents that particular aspect of consciousness against which energy can be created, or a push can be manifested. Let us return to the analogy of walking on ice in leather soles. When friction disappears, or at least when it is diminished to a great degree, it is hard to walk; in fact, it is hard to stand. If it is going to create and unfold the potentials that are within it by itself, spirit requires some kind of manifestation against which it can push to develop friction.

Occultly, friction is a concept which refers to the union of two forces which produces a third force, and it is that third force that is the power, the energy, the life. Spirit crystallises itself, changes itself into matter, and then uses that matter as a springboard into further creative unfoldment. Here arises a process of circulation. Spirit descends into matter, which is, simply, the crystallised manifestation of its creative impulse, so that it may experience that and push against the experience, in turn unfolding new visions and capacities which launch it into another creative cycle in which new matter is formed.

What happens to the old matter? It disintegrates and eventually returns to the level of spirit. So you have a continual cycle occurring. You have two forces at work. We call the first involutionary, the force that takes spirit on whatever level we find it and moves it to a lower density. This may not be matter as we understand it. It could be moving from a spiritual realm to a mental realm, or from a mental realm to an emotional realm, or from an emotional realm to a physical realm, but it is always a process of descent. Then there is the other process which is ascent, which is the return of matter into spirit. This works in two ways: in the release of new possibilities, and in the disintegration of matter which has been used up, matter which has fulfilled itself.

Both of these processes, the process of arising out of matter into new creative potential and realisation and the process of disintegrating used-up matter—if I may use such a term—back into primeval energy to be used again, are processes which create energy. They are processes which can be tapped. A consciousness can, as it were, align itself with either the forces which create involution and disintegration, or it can align itself with the forces that create evolution and transcendency.

Whether this is a good thing or not depends entirely on the quality and attunement of the consciousness that is doing the aligning. If its work at that moment is that of disintegrating matter or drawing something down into materialisation, then it is well and proper for it to align itself with those forces and intelligences that have that as their function. If the consciousness, however, is seeking to transcend matter and unfold new creative possibilities, then it would be inappropriate for it to attune to those intelligences of descent. It would be out of timing and out of place.

In the early days of human development upon the planet, the most vital forces for consciousness were the forces of descent. This was necessary, otherwise humanity could not have entered into materialised expression. There comes a time, however, when a switch-over takes place for each individual consciousness. If the consciousness does not make the switch from aligning with one energy to another, then it has problems. It has problems because part of its growth will continue in a way which is not designed for it, and part of its growth which should continue will not do so—a situation somewhat analogous to certain glandular deficiencies which create a strange physical effect.

Because human consciousness is a consciousness that seeks to attune to many levels of activity and intelligence, it must learn to identify with power in order to understand and be able to work with them. But if a being begins to identify strongly with that power which is wielded by the intelligences of either descent or disintegration, when that power is no longer appropriate, then we have the development of what is occultly known as a black magician.

All forms of evil in the world are manifestations of energy which is out of its proper point in the cycle of circulation. It can be beautiful energy, energy that is wonderful when utilised in its proper place; but utilised in the wrong place it can create chaos. It is like throwing a spanner in the works. It is like putting one of those metal rings from a beer can into a parking-lot meter. To a policeman, that is evil because it jams the parking-meter—and besides, the council does not get the money that it should be getting.

All energy and creation is God-manifested. It comes from God and is proper. Evil does not exist in any absolute sense. It does exist, however, through certain energies entering points of the cycle where they should not be. This comes about through a consciousness which is not in tune with the cycle. Any consciousness which, metaphorically speaking, cannot see past the end of its nose is open to manifesting evil.

Human consciousness is designed to experience separation, and from experiencing separation to grow back into a greater sense of oneness. Instead of being part of an amorphous oneness in which the being is at one with all things and therefore has nothing to create with, human consciousness has moved into a pattern of separation. I can illustrate this for you by using the life of a very wonderful person. This was Helen Keller, who, as a young child, had a disease which rendered her completely blind and deaf so that her main sensory contacts with the world were cut off. Through the efforts of her teacher, Annie Sullivan, she experienced one day an illumination in which she suddenly realised what all these tactile sensations that she was used to experiencing really meant. Suddenly she realised what abstractions were, and out of that she developed rapidly and went on to university. She became highly educated— you know the effect of her life.

Helen Keller did not passively absorb qualities and experiences from the world, because she was far more separated than most of us are; what she demonstrated was the quality of unfolding to the world something that was within. She had to find her creative sources within, because so much was blocked from outside of her. That is the position the human race is in. It has had certain psychic senses temporarily removed so that it has to evolve from within itself a realisation of the oneness of which it is a part. It has to create that oneness; for when you work for something, when you build or create something, it has far more meaning and power than if it is simply given to you.

Human consciousness has moved through separation to return to the oneness and to build a more powerful creative union with the divine than it would if that union was always there in consciousness. In so doing, it entered into matter and became part of this circulation of descent and ascent. The jeopardy of a separated consciousness is that, in the process of evolving from within itself a sense of unity, a sense of the unfolding microcosm, it goes through a period of selfishness. It has to do this. It has first to be brought to a point of self-consciousness before it can begin to function as a self-conscious being. That having been developed, it is necessary for it to release and move through that self-consciousness into an awareness of the whole, unifying it with the whole, this time in terms of a divine marriage—a creative coming together with the whole.

If this is not done, you have a situation in which the person is seeing things from the point of view of the microcosmic or strictly self-centred world. The energies being invoked and generated from within may be perfectly appropriate to the microcosmic world, but perfectly inappropriate to the macrocosmic or larger holistic cycle in which the person belongs. What is called 'evil' derives from this. A point was once reached where human consciousness was so busy functioning in a microcosmic or narrow sense that there were a lot of energies 'floating around' that had absolutely no reason for being where they were and when they were. Much of this limited expression has not been cleared, though there have been tremendous spiritual operations over the past two thousand years to absorb and put these energies back into their proper place.

Evil does not exist within the consciousness of the whole. A person whose consciousness is attuned to the whole does not see evil. But he or she can see energies that are out of time and out of place. By seeing them, that person can take steps to put them in their proper place without judging them or saying, "You are an evil energy"—without forming any kind of separation in his or her consciousness or conflict with the thing being dealt with.

A person's consciousness, if one is part of the whole, must in itself be whole. You cannot engage in separation within your consciousness by saying, "This I will accept, and that I will not accept." Instead you must say, "The whole accepts all things. Within my uniqueness there may be things that do not flow to me, which is all right; but I can see their rightness within their proper place and their proper time in the total scheme." I will use an illustration of this. Suppose a rattlesnake came wandering into the room. There are three ways we could deal with it. We could become excited and afraid, because we realise through past associations that this crawling thing upon the ground has the power to kill us. It is a dangerous animal. From that point of view we realise that this thing must be dealt with. We may go and kill it, or we may capture it, or we may do something else to it. As we attack the snake, it is going to see us and say, "Good grief! There is a dangerous animal called a human being," and it is going to do what it can to defend itself. So you have two things that are right in their own place coming into conflict.

Alternatively, I might see this thing and say, "Oh, that doesn't exist. There's no snake there. I refuse to accept that. All I see is that everything is all right." At which point the snake comes over and bites me. As I am dying, I am still afirming the all-rightness of everything.

But I may see the snake and recognise it for what it actually is: a living being for which I have no fear, only love. Yet I recognise that its being in a room crowded with people is likely to create bad situations. So I will take steps to put it where it belongs. I will put it outside, for example. There are people like this: there is one woman who works in one of our major zoos who is so attuned to animal life that she can walk into the reptile house and the snakes come up and cuddle her. It is hard to think of a reptile cuddling people, but she has a tremendous affinity for the life of these creatures. It is quite possible.

Our response to evil needs to be similar. Any energy we see that is what we call evil is simply energy that is out of place or out of timing, but it is perfectly all right in itself. It is like a square peg in a round hole. It may also be simply a projection of our own consciousness which says, "I'm uncomfortable with that particular thing, and I would prefer it not to be around." There are many things that we call evil that are not that at all, in any sense. They are in their right place, in their right timing, except that our consciousness does not perceive that. In either case, if we can raise our consciousness to a sense of the whole, a sense of oneness—peace, love, trust—then we see it in a different perspective. If we are at fault and are establishing a conflict that need not be there, then the conflict is resolved. If the energy is at fault and should not be there, we can take steps to remove it, to put it where it belongs; which is, in essence, redeeming it, putting it where it can do its thing, and hence we create blessing rather than confusion.

Some energies which are tapped are no longer useful any place on the Earth. They belong to a very ancient age of humanity's and Earth's manifestation, and they need to be returned to that ancient age. When the Great Invocation says, "May it seal the door where evil dwells," occultly what is meant by this is the sealing of some of the power-lines that were established long ago and which now represent leaks in the circulation system of the Earth's energy flows. This means nothing in terms of an absolute reality of evil. It only means that there is a leaky pipe somewhere in the circulation of the Earth's energies—a leaky pipe that has been gnawed at by some human consciousness in the past.

This leads us into the concept of healing. Healing, in terms of what we are, is an unreal concept. It presupposes a condition of unwholeness—but this can only develop where the consciousness is in a condition of unwholeness. Therefore ultimately all healing

29

must in some way transform consciousness. It must go to the root of the pattern, of the separation. It must restore to that consciousness its ability to do the right thing at the right time and be part of the circulatory pattern of its life and of the greater life of which it is a part.

However, if you went to a hungry man and started lecturing him on the fact that if he raised his consciousness he could manifest food, you would probably have very little luck. As long as his attention is focused on the fact that he has a "rumbly in his tumbly," as Winnie-the-Pooh says, he is not going to be very willing or able to lift his consciousness to some cosmic level which has no meaning for him. A piece of bread has far more meaning than an abstract teaching. Feed the man first and then you can approach him.

This is the position that healers are in. Ultimately, healing the physical form does nothing unless there is a complementary change of consciousness. All healers know this. If this does not take place, the physical form will return rather rapidly to the state it was in. It will most likely return to a worse state, because added to it will be that deeper sense of despair that, "I thought the thing had been taken care of and here it is again." People who divide their consciousnesses, once they have been integrated, have then the impact of knowing what has been lost because they have experienced it. That added impact can make things far worse for them. It is much better not to worry about it. If a person has lost it, that person will find it again. The secret of all healing is in the ability of the consciousness to relax and to flow and allow its fragmented parts to come back together again, which they will do quite naturally given half a chance.

We are now entering a new age. This age is going to demand from people different ideas and concepts. One concept which is undergoing change—and is at the root of such things as healing, and good and evil—is the concept of God.

How we conceive God organises the rest of our life patterns. If we think of God as that being, or presence, which is fighting evil in the universe, then we have no choice but to duplicate that in our lives and we too will be fighting things. If we cannot find anything to fight, we will project and create something, because we will not feel satisfied unless there is some negative presence in our environment to combat—if that is our consciousness.

On the other hand, if our concept of God is of a wholeness of which we are a part and which we experience, and the manifestation of divinity is that out-reaching force of love, truth, and light which perceives the wholeness and seeks always to manifest and exemplify it, then we are not functioning in terms of conflict. We are functioning in terms of placing things into their proper position, lovingly, truthfully, but without doing battle with them.

Healers, or people who are functioning in an occult or spiritual way, are as effective as their spiritual concepts allow them to be. There is an energy that can flow from the hands—a purely psychic (that is, etheric) energy that can flow and affect the physical body. It can heal the physical body. At some point, however, a change has to be wrought in the consciousness of the patient. The healers of the new age will be those people whose whole life is manifesting unity. They may not be looking upon themselves as being healers specifically. They will look upon themselves as being manifestations of the whole. From them will flow a force that is healing in a positive way because it is 'wholesome', and returns all things to the whole.

Many healers function on the level of the disease itself. This is the same as functioning on the level of the hunger, and this is quite proper. You have to give a starving man something to eat before you can meet him on another level of consciousness. If a person is convulsed with pain, do something to alleviate the pain. Don't sit and tell her to rise above the pain, because her consciousness may not be able to do that. However, people who are becoming at one with wholeness begin to radiate that wholeness with such power that they can literally take over the vehicles of the patients and impress upon them that peace, that new resonance which creates healing and alleviation.

I feel that we will move into a time when the light and love that will flow will create instantaneous healing in many cases. There is also something that the patients can do. If the patients can hold the consciousness of perfection, they will then demand from all who come to heal them that they hold the same consciousness. The patients will not allow anyone to work with them whose consciousness is less than attuned to the whole—because here again we run into this cycle of projection in which by recognising something as a separate reality in itself with its own kind of power, we give it that power.

I have encountered this on the inner level with some healers that I have met from time to time who are actually maintaining their patients in the disease pattern, but not entirely through their own consciousness or fault; it is just that that is where their consciousness is. The patients should surround themselves with that energy which lifts the consciousness of the healer. It has to be this two-way giving and receiving so that both are lifted. Again it is the analogy of the snake. If a person is in dis-ease, it is because some aspect of that person's consciousness, some aspect of his or her body, is out of rhythm, out of circulation with the whole. We can recognise that this is so. The power that flows from us should be the power of love, of wholeness.

I can point this out to you in terms of pain. When we have pain, it gnaws away at us. But pain is a blessed thing. Pain is only healthy tissue manifesting an informational communication. Diseased tissue does not hurt. It is healthy nerve tissue that is letting you know something is wrong. Pain is a signal; it is not a disease in itself. If you do not feel pain, then you are sick. If you have some form of disease and you are not feeling any pain, your informational system is not working. Pain is not an evil thing in itself. What it does do is to let us know that there is need for a change. If we then begin to make this change, the pain disappears. I have experienced this a number of times in my own life—suddenly having pain for no reason at all. Examining my pattern, seeing something that might be changed and changing it, the pain disappears. I find later that a possible physical condition has disappeared.

It is a healthy body that gets sick, that lets us know that it is sick. It is something like a fever; most of the symptoms that we actually experience are the healthy defense mechanisms of the body attempting to maintain the wholeness. The root-cause of the disease is something more subtle which may not actually be experienced. If our consciousness can move out of conflict or even help the mechanisms of the body into their proper flow within the wholeness, then we find that we generate an energy which assists us and assists anyone who comes in to heal us. Those who do come in to heal are greatly benefited by this assistance.

I said that this is true in most cases. There are those people who deliberately take on to themselves certain patterns of illness because of sacrificial reasons, reasons of transmutation. This will probably fade out in the future because there will not be much need for it, but it has been very evident in the past. It is difficult to heal these people because their consciousness itself is creating the condition. It is doing it because it has willed itself to do it, and because it is right for it to do it at that time. Until that force is released in consciousness, no healing is possible.

The new age represents a change of human consciousness in its relationship to the divine, in which it moves out of that consciousness in which it is separate from God and moves into that consciousness in which it is at one with God. From that consciousness it automatically becomes a source for the radiation of that wholeness in which no evil can exist, and in which only wholeness can be manifested. Anything which is dark is returned to its rightful place, at which point it ceases to be of the dark. Anything which is of illness is returned to its proper pattern, because it has been summoned back into its proper state and the wholeness has been re-established.

People who would be healers—who are healers—may have a tremendous flow through the body. In their consciousnesses, however, they should not think of themselves as healers, or indeed as anything separate from the wholeness. It is the wholeness, the oneness, that is the source of health, the source of right circulation. It is not an energy that is transmitted. It is not a force that we direct against anything. It is that continual radiation and resonance of the life which creates in all of its surroundings and all that comes into it a oneness which corresponds to the oneness radiated from the source of that life.

There are really two kinds of healing—two kinds of energies useful for healing on the physical levels. One is the energy that is generated through the physical body of the healer which may be stimulated by energies coming from higher levels, which moves out to bless and heal and restore the physical body of the patient to its perfect condition. But that is a form of alleviation and not a cure. Behind that and along with it there should be the important energy of realisation, within the consciousness of the healer, of the presence and reality of wholeness. It is not a question here of recognising or not recognising disease or evil or any of these opposites which we do not particularly like. It is a question of *how* we recognise them and what the consciousness is that perceives them. A great deal of difficulty has been created by people not recognising realities. When a plumber recognises a leaky valve, can I recognise it in the same way? Do I feel that the leaky valve is threatening my world? Or do I just see it as something that needs a little mending? Or do I recognise it in terms of conflict, or in terms of fear?

The forces of darkness have as much power as they do because we duplicate what they are within ourselves. We do this because the main sources of all darkness are fear and the concomitant aspects of anxiety, hatred and anger. When people use fear or hatred or anger or violence against fear or hatred or anger or violence, they have not really accomplished very much. They are only re-creating the situation they are fighting. If one is going to deal with the leaky faucets of consciousness and the misapplied energies of the world, then one's consciousness must be in a different state. One must not duplicate those energies within oneself. One *is* the cure, *is* the wholeness, *is* the answer. One is not applying a cure; not radiating or directing an answer. One *is* the cure.

On the level of energy flow, the actual mechanism of all healing takes place through changes in energy, effected or complemented by changes in consciousness. We know that colour and music have a direct effect on the physical body. It has been demonstrated that certain glandular activities are either augmented, stimulated, subdued or depressed by the presence or absence of certain colours. If you walk into the presence of red, your pulse goes up and your respiration increases. If you come into the presence of blue, your pulse rate decreases, your respiration decreases. The same is true of certain kinds of music: they can be used to form the environment in which energies can flow most properly. What we are trying to do in most kinds of healing is to create a state of relaxation and release within the patients so that they can attune to the healing energies that are normally within themselves. It is the stress and the tension being maintained through the consciousness of the individual that is blocking the flow, congesting the cycle. If the manifestation of certain music and colour can calm this down and create an environment in which greater flow can tak place, then this is one way in which they will work.

There are other ways, too. Colour and music are definite manifestations of energy, and some healers are using music, not so much to relax a person but in a way where different sounds are attuned to different kinds of diseases. When that sound is reproduced, it sets up a resonation within the organ in question which will create a healed condition. I know one woman in America who was doing this through a process she called 'toning', in which she would teach a person to go up and down musical scales, not attempting to sing them but just letting the voice rise and fall; and the voice would, after a while, naturally rest on one note. She would then sound that note, and this had healing effects within the individual.

34

What will probably evolve is the use of the energies inherent in colour and sound to focus them directly on various patterns of disease or darkness, to transmute them, to restore the balance as it should be. Once the balance is restored the darkness cannot exist there; it is automatically returned to wherever it came from.

Chapter Four
DRUGS IN THE NEW AGE

ALL PATTERNS in the world today must be looked upon in relationship to a central event occuring at this time in human and planetary history. This event is the introduction of a new age, the arising within the planetary awareness of a recognition and a reception of a new kind of energy. This can be seen from a scientific basis; it can be seen from a spiritual basis; it can be seen as the movement of the Earth and the rest of the solar family into new cosmic relationships. It may also be seen as the movement of human consciousness, under the impact of swifly arising new challenges and experiences, into a new realm of perception and behavior.

If new consciousness and new behaviour is not formulated and expressed, homo sapiens and several other species upon the Earth will cease to exist as physical entities. Therefore as we approach this time, we call it a new age in that a turning point has been reached, and nothing upon the planet will ever be the same again.

In terms of consciousness this is creating a tremendous urge toward greater freedom, greater creative expression and greater realisation of human identity. The human race has used up the frontiers of the Earth: no longer is there any place to which to migrate. The new frontiers are either under the ocean or in outer space, and both require great expenditures of finance, energy and technology to explore, which for the most part are beyond the capacity of any one nation. Therefore these are not yet valid frontiers. Instead, there is the frontier of human consciousness to begin to explore and externalise: new potentials, new possibilities, new powers hidden within the human psyche.

This frontier can be regarded as being a psychological movement towards a greater understanding of human potential, particularly as expressed in that brand of psychology known as 'self-actualising psychology', in which the task of the psychologist is to research and explore potentials within the human being and to help people express themselves with greater sensitivity and awareness.

This frontier can also be seen in a spiritual fashion as the movement of consciousness and life into another dimension of expression, freeing it from the gravity of a lower density and allowing it to perceive and respond to higher vibrational modes of life. However we choose to look upon it, it is a motion away from the restricted and restricting modes of life that are symbolised by density, matter, tradition, the past or 'the establishment'. It is a movement towards greater freedom and less imposed limitations upon people's ability to express themselves freely.

The drug scene must be looked upon in terms of this motion in human consciousness, this new age arising. Throughout history, drugs have been used to elevate consciousness beyond a state of perception and realisation conditioned by gravity, density, space and time, and by the limitations of society. This approach has been for mystical reasons, spiritual reasons, or reasons of pure escape. The individuals who cannot run away physically from the patterns that bond them can run into themselves through many means: through losing themselves in physical activity, emotional activity, mental activity; through drink, through drugs.

In recent years the drug pattern emerged as a definite tool to allow individuals to liberate themselves from the binding consciousness of the personality, of social awareness, of dense, physical awareness, and to soar into greater heights of perception, sensitivity and creativity. For many people the experience has been mystical: it has been transcendental and very positive.

A drug is simply a tool. If properly developed and produced, the natural drugs which are hallucinogenic do not have adverse effects upon the physical body. Whether they are positive or negative in their ultimate effects on the personality is largely dependent on the motives and structure of that personality when the drug is taken. Many modern drugs, however, are not natural. They are not prepared carefully; they are synthetic, or else embody a vibrational pattern which is more powerful than the personality can withstand.

Most drugs which people have used through the centuries are natural substances derived from plants, like mushrooms and various fungi. Many of them are quite poisonous unless treated. One of the problems in the past that made drug use less prevalent was the fact that a person taking drugs was just as likely to die as to have a transcendental experience. LSD is a natural substance, for example, which is also poisonous unless it is properly treated. It has been used by people for centuries but has often induced death through poisoning, just as many mushrooms have.

A person is a manifestation of intelligence on several levels. One's body has intelligence; one's soul has intelligence. The body pattern represents various intelligent lives manifesting themselves as the cellular patterns, the pattern of the organs, tissue, and so forth—all brought together within one over-riding integrative life which we will call the etheric body. This flows from the life and intelligence of the soul itself and impresses upon the multitude of minor lives a certain unifying principle, which enables the physical body to manifest as an organism and not as a community of independent cells. This integrative life has its own pattern of direction, its own powers, its own potentials. If it is attuned to the higher nature and is drawing direction and potential from that source, then its power is vastly increased, for it is multi-dimensional in its impact and not simply physical in its reality.

All drugs represent a manifestation of an intelligence. They represent a certain pattern of forces, of energies moving in a direction and with a power determined by their own intelligence. If you combine a drug, any drug, with a living body, you are combining two intelligences, two forces. If one is stronger than the other, it will become dominant.

Humanity is in a unique position because its physical intelligence is weakened and modified by the necessity for that intelligence to blend with higher spiritual levels. In cases where human physical or instinctual intelligence is too powerful, the higher levels cannot properly influence, and we say "there is an individual who is too tied into the physical realm." Even for an individual of that nature, however, there is a limit beyond which animal intelligence cannot go in terms of manifesting its own power and identity.

When a drug is introduced, its intelligent power is measured against the intelligent power of the body. If it is less, then the body's direction maintains itself, although it may do so with some difficulty and tension. If the pattern of the drug is greater, then the intelligence of the drug will take control. This can cause disruption and complete disintegration of the body's forces, which results in death or in a severe loss of the body's ability to function as an integrative structure—for example, paralysis, disease, or disruption of the central nervous system.

38

People respond to drugs differently depending on the amount of body intelligence which they have. A drug which cannot impose itself strongly upon one person because of that person's natural physical resiliency and resistance may become a dominant factor and impose itself very severely upon another individual whose resistance is less.

We have a natural tendency to separate into the component parts of body, mind, emotion, and spirit. It takes a true effort on the part of people's spiritual intelligence to maintain the links that allow the integrative phenomenon that is a human being to express itself. This is why sleep is important. Sleep is the process in which the being separates itself into its component parts for relaxation and recharging. A person who does not sleep for long periods of time begins to disintegrate on all levels, because the energies which synthesise his various component levels of intelligence weaken and those levels begin to move apart into competing expressions.

Anything which introduces added stress into the system of a human being threatens this integrative process and increases the tendency that separation will occur. It is like a mixture of salad dressing, in which the oil and vinegar and other things separate unless there is a continual motion to shake it up and keep them mixed. Separation for a human being means that the spiritual patterns move to their level, the physical patterns move to their level, the emotional patterns move to their level, and so forth. They no longer cooperate, and even communication between these levels may be severely impaired.

When a person takes a drug, it introduces into the physical pattern added forces which physical energy must cope with. The physical pattern must concentrate its intelligence upon this foreign entity which has entered and come to terms with it in some way. But this releases the integrative forces and allows the spiritual patterns to move to their own level. This is why the drug pattern has been used to effect transcendental experiences, because it does have this separating effect.

It can be said that it causes the etheric body to move out of the physical, but that is only a minor phenomenon. What actually happens is that it causes a concentration of physical energy within the physical body, something analogous to the state a person is in after eating a heavy meal. The consciousness is fogged because the blood moves from the brain down to the stomach. The introduction of a drug causes energy to move from higher levels—from the work of maintaining the integrative links—down to the physical level to take care of this problem. Fasting does exactly the same thing. Disease can do the same thing. Pain can do the same thing by focusing energy onto the physical, which causes the higher levels to separate and move back to their vibrational homeland.

But some links remain. If they did not, death would occur. Through these links the personality experiences what it calls transcendental phenomena. The problem arises if no form of integrative effort is made to tie the pure experience of transcendental phenomena meaningfully into the whole life pattern—physically, emotionally, mentally and spiritually—so that it adds to the integrative force of the being. A purely phenomenal experience does not have the power to do this. If the phenomenal experience has been reached through a reduction of the integrative power and presence, it simply exists as a crystallised experience. It may be beautiful. It may be meaningful in certain limited terms, but it is not ultimately meaningful—it represents a crystallised deposit within the consciousness.

At some point the integrative faculties have to deal with this. Either the experience becomes part of the total life stream, adding to the communication and the communion of all the levels in that unity that we know of as human life, or it remains as a lump, a deposit, like a calcium deposit in the blood stream. If the experiences are continued and not integrated, the deposits build up and build up until through cumulated effect the integrative power of the life is broken down and we have an individual who is disoriented, confused, unable to focus one's energies properly and unable to find any meaningful direction for one's life.

Drugs are not the only thing that will cause this. Many forms of spiritual discipline will cause it as well, if these disciplines do not include the power of the integrative or Christ-life. Fasting, yoga, meditation—anything which seeks to pit one level against another and does not in some way create a meaningful experience that ties all the levels together into an integrated unity will create the same effect, although perhaps not as quickly or as dramatically as drugs will do. Here we are dealing with a very wide-spread phenomenon which must not be limited to drugs alone.

If a person under the influence of drugs, fasting, yoga, meditation, pain, whatever stimulus it may be, has an experience and is powerful enough in one's integrative faculties to draw that experience in and make it one with oneself rather than allowing it to remain simply an experience, and if it is looked upon as being part of that oneness, then positive effects will result. But most human beings do not have that kind of integrative power. They are working at peak capacity just to maintain themselves on a human level, and the weariness that they feel is seen in their desire to escape, through popular literature, television, cinema, drugs, sex, or any other form of ego-diversion.

There exists within the being of such people a continual state of integrative fatigue. There is literally no meaning, no vision, and no purpose in their lives with which to increase their integrative faculties. What we mean when we talk about this faculty is the *Logos power* within the individual, the power to give meaning and wholeness to life.

Within the new age the tendency is to move beyond density. It is to escape gravity and all its implications. This movement must be done in a unified way, however, so that the Logos power of the being is maintained and the various aspects of intelligence do not fly apart at random. There is a necessity to move from one dimension of experience to another, and drugs will seemingly give this effect. They do give this effect—they liberate the higher faculties—but they do not reunite them with the Logos presence which is the key divinity of the individuality. As a consequence they give the semblance of new age satisfaction, of moving into a higher level, but it is not real unless the experience has become integrated and unified. Hence the total result of drugs and other patterns of escape or of 'spiritual sensuality' is likely to maintain the being not in a new age state but in one of cumulative disintegration.

Humanity's need is to integrate itself, which means human beings cannot pit one level of consciousness or intelligence against another. They must, if they are going to move into a higher level, take their Earth level with them. If they do not do this, they miss the whole point of what the new age is about. Instead of enhancing their creative capacities, they diminish them and place themselves in a process of disintegration which will ultimately result in death—sometimes the worst kind of death, a living death in which the person is for all practical purposes a zombie without any true directive capacity operating through its personality. It is necessary for people to maintain contact with Earth—not to escape or leave it, but to maintain increased contact to counterbalance the increased energies that are bringing about the new age.

There is an analogy to this in voice training. If people want to reach a higher note in singing, there are two ways to do it. They can strain their voices to reach this high note, in which case they may reach it but it will sound strained. Their voices will become fatigued and they will be unable to maintain the power to continue singing at that level. Voice instructors, however, teach a different method. When you are reaching for a high note, you do not think of the high note; you think of the same note in lower octaves, and imagine yourself not as reaching the high note but of pulling the high note down, deep into the abdominal cavity. This does work. It enables the individual to reach very high notes without any strain upon the voice because the effort is being pulled down and anchored into a lower level of the physical body.

Exactly the same thing is required in the new age. We cannot strain towards the higher levels. We must anchor ourselves firmly into the lower levels and pull the higher levels down so that at all times the Logos—the integrative faculty—is maintained. High and low are brought closer into oneness, and are not allowed to spread apart.

This has meaning in terms of the treatment of drug problems. A person who has been taking drugs and thereby has become separated within will find that integrative faculties have been reduced and the various levels of consciousness are now functioning in a more independent way. This can be giving that person what is called 'highs', or phenomenal experiences; but occultly they represent a waste of energy unless in some way this experience is brought within a disciplined focus and expressed through a unified being. It is not experience that we are seeking. The thing to do for a person who has been on drugs is in some way to restore that person's integrative power and to reinforce and restrengthen it. Since the effect of a drug is generally to place the higher and lower levels on their different vibrational levels, increasing the gap between them, the person should be placed into some kind of an environment that draws the two back together. One of the environments that is most ideally and naturally suited to this is the soil.

It has been known for centuries in psychic and occult circles that if people who have been projecting themselves out of their bodies, or have been engaged in occult research on the inner planes or in psychic manifestations, and for some reason have become fatigued or are unable to re-enter their bodies adequately, they

42

should immediately move out into intimate physical contact with the soil—through working in a garden, or planting, or by some form of physical labor; something which places them in contact with natural forces. The power of the Logos is moving throughout the Earth, and people must maintain their attunement with it. This is one reason why people who take drugs within a purely natural surrounding tend to have less of a problem than people who take drugs in a city. There the Logos power of the Earth has been displaced by the artificiality of human creations, which generally do not express this integrative quality but rather a multitude of isolated qualities, all competing for a person's attention.

I envision drug treatment centres concentrating on or developing around gardens, farms and places where physical labour can be achieved in a relaxed and therapeutic environment. The food should nourish the being in the body and strengthen the intelligence of the physical body, because with the drug still present or residual in the bloodstream, and with the higher faculties separated, the intelligence of the physical body is weakened and its direction scattered. This could be combined with some form of education which presents new vision to the person, and perhaps some form of psychological therapy to resurrect within the individual a sense of meaning in that person's life and in the world. All of this strengthens the Logos quality which is the only quality, ultimately, that can counteract the power of drugs.

Even a minor drug like marijuana can have a disintegrating effect. If its intelligence is greater than the intelligence of the person taking it, its effect can be just as potent for that person as heroin may be for another. Chemical drugs—synthesised drugs which are not natural in origin—have an even more potent effect because they introduce totally alien foreign elements. The body can at least cope with natural drug forms to some degree, because it recognises certain natural affinities. But unnatural drugs, synthetic drugs, even things like aspirin, tranquillisers and pain-killers, introduce totally alien elements into the body, and because of this add increased stress to the integrative qualities of the being.

The problem for humanity is not one of drugs. It is a problem of lack of vision, lack of that integrative quality which could override and place it superior to the many kinds of intelligence within our world that clamour for people's attention and which would give them the ability to cope with modern stress. People become addicted to external intelligences like alcohol, drugs, television, gurus, spiritual techniques, and certain social patterns, because they have no counterbalancing intelligence or Logos within themselves which can manifest their own unique identity in a positive fashion.

Humanity's basic problem is one of addiction. Addiction is simply the giving over of the Logos quality of the being to an external intelligence so that the being is supported by that external intelligence. People can be addicted to many things. They can be addicted to a God-image, to a guru-image, to an organisational-image, to drugs, to alcohol, to anything that robs them of their individual creativity.

A drug pattern must therefore be seen in its larger aspects—not as an isolated problem but as part of a human condition which needs to be dealt with at this time. The way to deal with it is to provide people with creative opportunities, for example, training them to produce things on their own. Some form of artistic or craft discipline would certainly help people who are into drugs. Contact with the soil—because of its healing elements—and contact with nature are important; as is contact with some educative force which works to build within the individual a greater realisation of one's own inner Logos presence, one's divine and creative power.

Humanity is entering a new age. This stimulates a tendency to move into higher dimensions, and people respond to this by seeking ways of entering those dimensions. Drugs help them to do this. Spiritual techniques may help them to do this. Fasting may help them to do this. They all do it in a way which if not combined with an increase in one's Logos power creates the sensation of arising but the reality of separation. The higher beings move to their level, the lower beings move to their level—and the phenomenon that is experienced by the personality may be one of considerable beauty or emotional satisfaction, but very little usefulness in terms of the evolution of the soul. The entire pattern must be lifted: Earth as well as heaven, body as well as consciousness, emotion as well as the higher levels of supermind and spirit.

The drug pattern has many good effects. This cannot and should not be denied. For those people whose integrative faculties are powerful, it has good effects. When one is taking a drug, however, one is always engaging in a test of strength with an alien intelligence. If one comes out on top, one may have a greater experience, a greater life from it; but one has done so by placing oneself in jeopardy. If our own powers are at any time weakened or at any time drained off because of external conditions, and the intelligence of the drug is stronger, we will find ourselves mastered by that intelligence, with grave results.

The thing that must now be given to people in new age teaching is freedom from all forms of addiction, and from seeking external aid to replace the internal power that is there. External aids can always help, but only if they increase and augment people's integrative capacities and creative powers. People may be prevented from moving into the drug pattern by education, through building for them new vision and giving their lives new meaning. People who are on drugs may be helped by placing them into creative, therapeutic environments, close to nature, where they are given opportunities to build and express their creative powers—perhaps through wood-carving, painting, or modelling with clay—where that involves a discipline to tie the being back together.

The drug pattern will diminish as we help human consciousness to realise the revelation of its own capacities. Therefore I see it as primarily an educational problem. It is inevitable that it occurs at this time. Humanity is seeking to expand its consciousness, but it must be given a new vision of how to do it and what this expansion really means. It is not the experience of higher levels that is sought, but expansion of the creative and integrative faculties which make all levels one and allow that oneness to express in perfect attunement to the needs of the whole and in revelation of one's personal and unique divinity.

This is the true expansion, not of consciousness but of identity and of meaning and of universal life. As more and more people become aware of this and are led into attunement with it, all forms of addiction will change. Spiritual teachings and organisations will alter themselves. People will not be so dependent on external leaders. Drugs, alcohol—all of these patterns will change as humanity begins to unfold in its consciousness a greater realisation of purpose in life, and of people's creative powers to fulfil that purpose.

Chapter Five
CYBERNETICS AND SOCIETY IN THE NEW AGE

NO ASPECT of human society, no problem of the human condition, can be seen in an isolated state. It can only be considered in relation to the whole of human development and consciousness; otherwise what are created are fragmented answers which create further difficulties. To consider the question of automation, factories, industrial manifestations in the new age, we have to consider it from the point of view of human evolution of consciousness and the fulfilment of human destiny.

One of the basic challenges is right use of energy. People are always receiving energy. They are unfolding it from many levels— physically, emotionally, mentally—and from the higher levels as well. But humanity is not an infinite reservoir of containment. It also has to express this energy and give it release. There is a law of circulation that demands a flow in and out.

One of the ways in which people have expressed energy in the past is through labour and through work. They have used these as a means of producing other energy, of producing the necessities for survival. That is, people work in order that they may live. Our entire economic system is based on the principle of people receiving the necessities of life in return for various energies that they pour out into the communal whole, however that whole is manifested, whatever the economic or political scheme may be for a particular country.

This in itself is a fundamental premise which is challenged by the new age. One of the essences of new age consciousness is that people do not have to work to receive the basic necessities of life such as food, clothing, shelter and what they require to survive. The potential exists within expanded consciousness literally to manifest these particular necessities supposedly out of thin air. Of course nothing comes out of nothing, but, utilising the laws of mind and spirit, people can create through crystallisation manifestations of things which are required. How long it takes for that kind of consciousness to manifest on a mass level is unknown. It will probably begin to manifest and is actually already manifesting on an individual level, but the number of people who can perform these apparently miraculous acts will undoubtedly remain small compared with the mass of humanity.

The principle is the same, however. People have looked upon work and labour as a means of sustaining themselves; but this is actually not the divine purpose of labour, which is to provide increasingly creative outlets for the energy people receive so that it flows in such a way that they are expanded, are able to grow, are able to unfold further aspects of themselves. In a way people do have to work harder or work more in order to receive; but what they are receiving in this case is an expanded realisation of the potentials that lie within them.

We do hold now the potential to create a society in which no human being would have to work to provide for oneself the necessities of life. The question is: is it proper to create this kind of society at the present time?

The basic problem for the human race is how to use energy. If the normal channels of energy-use are taken from it without their being replaced in some way in its consciousness with other channels, humanity will find itself in a very frustrating position; and this energy of frustration will create a distortion which will cause the energy people receive to be turned' back upon themselves or turned upon society in a destructive fashion, simply because the energies have no place to go. They are out of place and out of timing.

This is the situation that results with individuals who are trained in a given field and replaced by automation. Either because of their age, or because of their unwillingness to do so, or because of social factors, they find themselves unable to take up a new creative life— even if their earlier life had been rather hum-drum and they had been performing routine tasks. Their consciousness had moved into that particular groove, and it was providing an outlet for the release of energy.

People must be assisted to know how to express themselves creatively, how to find viable and proper substitutes for work, before work can be taken from them. Eventually, work only for the purpose of survival will disappear because that is the pattern of the new age. It is not a person's destiny to have to struggle to survive. There is other work, there are other challenges of consciousness which are far more vital and important. A whole universe awaits with unlimited creative possibilities.

47

Human consciousness needs to be changed and lifted above the level of the economic pattern, which says a person works to receive the energy to survive so that through that survival one can work to receive more energy to survive, and so on. Until that consciousness has changed, within the adjustment period there will have to be at least a comparable motion of consciousness, attitude and development toward creating for humanity a living and useful vision, and avenues of practical work that people can do, that will take the place of the ordinary job patterns that can be replaced by machinery.

We now have on an unprecedented scale the capacity to automate and to free people from having to provide the necessities of life. Yet there is this question of just what are the necessities of life. It would be ultimately self-defeating to remove from people the opportunity to work if this was not replaced with something equally creative and important. It is not enough just to make busy work for someone or to attempt to have one fill one's time with things which are of little importance—which in essence is what our society is seeking to do through its overwhelming emphasis on consumerism, turning the human consciousness into simply a response mechanism that buys and works so it can buy more without any real growth and meaning coming out of this process.

There are tremendous spiritual energies that have linked up with technological progress; but that progress must proceed in balance with the growth of human consciousness, the growth of the ability to handle time and the ability to see humanity in a perspective where it can use time creatively and in a worthwhile fashion, in a way that is satisfying to people as human beings.

When I was in college, my roommate was a young man from West Africa who was studying Agricultural Science. I remember his getting into a discussion with various American students who felt that what his country needed was for America to send over more tractors and automated machinery because it could take over the whole farming of his country and do it more efficiently and faster. He argued against this. He said they would much rather put 10,000 tribesmen to work with pickaxes, because then each individual would have something to do that was helping the country, rather than have those 10,000 tribesmen sitting on city streets with nothing to do. This is the problem of human consciousness not being ready at this point for the tremendous release from work that is developing through technological progress.

The value of Findhorn and comparable centres is if they can provide a meaningful alternative to work, something that the average individual can understand and deal with; then they help to lay the foundation on which a sacred automated society could be erected.

Looking some distance into the future, we can see that an automated society will eventually become unnecessary, because everything that a machine can do the human consciousness can do far better. Human consciousness has to be expanded and tuned into its cosmic levels of awareness, at which point—as far as the physical level is concerned—all powers of materialisation are laid open to it. Until that point is reached, however, we do have in the utilisation of computer technology and automation a possibility of releasing people from various patterns that are holding their consciousnesses in bondage.

This development of automation is one of those qualities that, like nuclear energy, like the population explosion, like pollution, is an evolutionary test of human consciousness. It is literally forcing upon people a re-evaluation of their status and position in creation. The factor of leisure time is a quality every bit as potent, in some ways far more destructively potent, than nuclear energy, simply because people have never in history been faced on a mass level with the challenge of leisure time, of not having to work—of finding that an empty day is before them and they have to fill it. People have not explored the depths of themselves and do not know how to draw out from themselves the qualities that will fill that day, that will produce a creative blending between the human consciousness and the consciousness of time.

A pattern I do see emerging as one of many alternatives being projected onto human consciousness, is the pattern of decentralisation, of moving people out of cities into small communal patterns. This can now be done without entering into tribal states because of the technology of communication that can link communities together, and the rapidity of modern transportation. A small community is no longer isolated geographically as it once was.

A small community can provide the advantages of close personal contact, personal work, or doing in a creative way things the community needs that a machine could do. A person could build a house and make it unique; or could help someone to prepare a garden, or what have you. There are many creative opportunities in small communities.

There is a motivation today towards a greater humanism, away from machines, and there is a comparable motivation towards greater cybernetic expression. Both of these are equally valid. They are both under hierarchical direction and are both divinely inspired. In some way a blend between them has to be found. However the question is settled, it has to be settled in a way that answers the basic need of people to have a valid creative outlet for all the energy that they draw into themselves, an outlet that has a meaning and gives life meaning, and allows people to unfold their divine potential.

Any other solution will be incorrect from an evolutionary standpoint and will not work. It will not last because human consciousness will rebel against it. A totally automated society, without comparable change in human consciousness to deal with it, would be a great evil. On the other hand, the present human society, where humanity is a slave to an economic condition which need not exist, should not exist and does not have to exist, is in itself an evil.

DISCUSSION

Q. Will factories be part of some of these communal centres like Findhorn in the future?

A. It would depend on the consciousness of the centre itself and just what it was attempting to manifest. There are many people who are highly attuned to the consciousness that is expressing itself in machines. That is their creative expression, and if that is so, their kind of community could very easily find its creative outlet in the work with machines.

I confess to a love where computers are concerned, because my father's work is in the field of computer science and some of the things that he is working with are fascinating and highly creative. Some of the things that are capable of being done now with computers go beyond what you read in science fiction. I can well understand individuals finding great creative outlet there; but there are other individuals who could not care less, and they would not want that kind of expression around them.

As far as Findhorn goes, it is certainly a possibility. This being a prototype centre, there is every possibility that this could develop, and you would be asked to find the reality of the Christ expression through cybernetic manifestation. God is there. We cannot say that that is not a divine expression, because it is. We need to know how to utilise it in a way that a person's divinity and a machine's divinity are released in a complementary fashion. This may be something that would develop at Findhorn.

Q. If machines are extensions of people and people are an extension of God, then machines are extensions of God. Does this affect how we use them?

A. There is another factor involved here which is found in the evolution of matter itself. It is the principle that all matter is intelligent. It has life, it has intelligence. There is an intelligence within machines, but it is a rather new intelligence, something that people are actually bringing into manifestation through their creation of machines. They are providing the means by which certain intelligences involved in matter can enter into a creative cooperative expression with people.

It is similar to the relationship that exists between human beings and their domestic animals. From an occult standpoint, through association with people their consciousness is helped to evolve. The same is true with certain energies involved in physical matter—metal, earth and plastic, for example. There is intelligence there, and through the relationship of person and machine there will be evolution on both sides. People will see certain aspects of themselves which they will come to understand more clearly and master; at the same time they will be releasing potentials of expression such as intelligence, cooperation, love and service within machines.

You have an example of that with the printing press at Findhorn. It will work only for certain people. This machine is quite sensitive to the consciousness of the operator and only certain people can use it. If anyone else tries to use it, even if they are skilled, the machine will not function properly.

In terms of the development of the race, it is considered at the present time that the key area of human development for the past two thousand years, and to some extent for the next two thousand years, is that of mind, and machines actually represent the externalisation of mental principles—especially computers. Most machines represent the externalisation of various characteristics of the mind, such as a certain rigidity, compartmentalisation, and a definite form of action. In creating a machine-society, humanity is creating something which is reflecting back to it its own mental evolution.

The problem there is that the machine can actually manifest mind in a purer form than people can do at the present time. A computer can out-think the human being because it is specialised. We find this in the nature kingdom. Humanity itself is a blend of all the kingdoms; but if a person runs into a fire elemental, we have a pure form which is far more powerful in its purity than that person in that particular aspect, although the human being is more powerful in terms of its ability to combine many aspects, which this other being cannot do.

We are now at a point where humanity's mind evolution has produced a machine culture which could conceivably be a source of power greater than its ability to control it. It is one of the problems you were talking about: people becoming slaves to the machine. Here we may introduce a factor of the new age which is the intuitive consciousness, which no machine can ever reproduce because it is on an entirely different level of manifestation. It is not a form or form-oriented consciousness. It operates on a causal level of pure energy and concept, and it is humanity's expansion into intuitive levels which will augment its mental power, allow it to develop a machine world but at the same time remain greater than it.

This is why development of an expanded intuitive consciousness is necessary in order for people to keep one step ahead of the things they are creating. What they are creating represent specialised manifestations of themselves, which in their speciality reflect back to them more power than they have or know they have within themselves; and these could conceivably put a person under their control.

As humanity begins to unfold a greater realisation of its infinite potentials, it can work with all these patterns and they will not be able to dominate it. It is all happening in a very right way. The timing is just perfect for all this, as of course it would need to be.

52

In many ways people's machine culture will help them to develop an expanded consciousness. It is having an evolutionary impact on humanity. It cannot help but have. It is forcing people to change their consciousnesses and their ideas, and out of this change comes the possibility of a more expanded awareness. Some people will change into a greater dependency on machines. Other people—if they do not just try and throw the whole thing out from a complete reaction against it—can move with it and take the benefits from it and move on to more expanded levels. They will find the perfect capacity to use a cybernated society without being dominated by that society.

Chapter Six
ECONOMICS AS A WAY OF THE SPIRIT

I AM NOT an economist, but I am very interested in ourselves as spiritual beings and as physical beings attempting to function with wisdom, with balance and with wholeness. I would like to begin by talking about the way of the spirit and use that as my lead-in to a consideration of economics.

Consider what the challenges of the spirit may be. Consider yourself as a being of infinite potential and possibility. Consider yourself as an inexhaustible oil-field. You are the source of energy, not its consumer.

You are then faced with two particular problems: first, how to be a human being who is a focused, finite, personalised, partial expression of your wholeness; second, how to be a human being on the planet Earth—which means having to take into account the will and directives of this world, what it is trying to achieve.

The human species fulfils a function within the beingness of our planet. When I as a soul attempt to relate to this world and to incarnate a 'persona'—when I am attempting as a soul to establish my 'branch office' down here—I must take into account the conditions that make this branch office necessary. What is the spirit of the Earth attempting to do?

One way of looking at this is to say that our world is attempting to individualise itself. I am drawing on a human psychological analogy by which we learn to become thinking, reasoning, wilful, aware, loving, wise, whole, functioning individuals, and am suggesting that our planet may be going through a very similar kind of process. Our particular part of that process we call human history and human evolution.

I do not want to make all this too esoteric, but simply suggest that one of the experiences of the human species is to learn to think on behalf of our planet, or to think on behalf of wholeness. So there is a pressure upon the human species which does not originate from within itself. It is not something we are doing to ourselves as much as it is something which is happening within us and

54

to us as a species, as part of an evolving world; and that is to learn how to think, act, feel and *be* in a state of wholeness with each other and with our planet.

Within that framework my soul faces the challenge of individualising itself through me, so that in some fashion David Spangler becomes a reasonably well-focused, well-balanced, well-manifested expression of this greater energy—and can do so in a way that fulfils not only his own personal needs, but also the needs of his species and of his world.

My soul is involved, therefore, in a process of economics. It is involved in the task of taking a certain amount of energy, working with it to externalise a human individuality, and setting up a resonance between me and itself so that there is a flow of energy, a flow of being, a flow of life between us. Hopefully, this investment of its energy in relationship to the Earth and the environment will generate enough profit, enough overflow, that it can relate to other people in a way that fulfils the desires, the will and the purposes of Earth.

The soul is attempting to externalise us as points of focus within the body of the Earth. The Earth is attemptint to externalise us as something like cells in the brain—a point relating to other points to create a larger whole. I call that process 'universalisation'. There is an impulse acting upon us to moderate our individuality in order that we can then relate without barriers, enabling us eventually to begin thinking, feeling, and acting in resonance in order to manifest the wholeness of this world. This does not mean that we will all think, feel, or act the same, but that whatever our thoughts, feelings, and actions are they will come out of a resonating commonality.

Here a subtle balance is required between the forces of individualisation and the forces of universalisation. If I become too individualised, I may become so bound up with the forces of my particular focus—forces of desire, forces of self-identification, all the economics of building a self and establishing boundaries between my self and the 'not self'—that those boundaries become a fortress to me and I become isolated.

On the other hand, I may become so attuned to planetary process, to the universalising processes, that I do not become a truly individuated person. My edges are too fuzzy, or certain parts of me are incomplete. I may be very developed on mental levels, but not very developed emotionally, or vice versa. I may be wholly a thinker, but not very much a doer, or vice versa. I may tune in to an energy of outpouring, planetary bliss and good fellowship, where I am very open to the forces of group-think, but do not manifest myself as an individual thinker, feeler and actor. I may simply sway like a seaweed with the currents of whatever thoughts and feelings are moving through my society or my planet. At the extreme, I may simply bliss out into the realms of spiritual glory and lose touch with the reality of being a human being.

So the challenge of my soul is to strike a balance between the energies of individualisation and the energies of universalisation. How to be limited and limitless at the same time—this is the basic, paradoxical challenge of my soul.

In the spiritual traditions, the human soul goes through a process of involution where its primary interest is to accumulate what it needs in order to have definition and individual beingness. Then it reaches the bottom of that involutionary swing and begins to move to where that individuality becomes synthesised within itself. It becomes nourished, it becomes dynamic, and then, like a seed, it wants to unfold, to give. This is like people who have a great 'need' for wealth and who put all their energy into success, accumulate money, possessions, literally condense themselves into consumption and ownership. Finally they are satiated and reach a point where this no longer fulfils them. They begin to become unattached, to use their wealth; they want to give it away, invest it, release themselves of possessions and become freer, more mobile, more expansive.

Hold, for a moment, these images of the soul as meeting this challenge of finding the middle path between creating a focus through which it can function, and yet allowing that focus in turn to be part of a universalising principle, part of a larger world to which it owes its energy and from which it receives energy. It is an economic unit in the broadest possible sense.

Let us now shift our attention to something that deals more directly with economic experience as we usually think of that term, in the sense of a financial relationship. In the United States I had the pleasure of working with a group called Community Service Incorporated, which was founded by Arthur Morgan, one of the leading figures in American education. He was president of Antioch College, which has the reputation of an open and progressive educational philosophy. Arthur Morgan was profoundly disturbed at the destruction of small communities, and at the concentration of power, finance, capital and personnel in cities, large corporations and conglomerates. What he was observing was the impact of the process of universalisation, the unfoldment of a new level of social reality out of a previous level which had been characterised by the village, the small community and the small town. He described the impact of nationalisation upon these small units in a number of works, one of which is called *The Simplicity of Economic Reality.*

He saw this process as one in which what had been an individual focus—the identity of the community—was exposed to the next level of universalisation—the nation and the planet—through national advertising, through national currencies, through things like the stock market, all of which had a dispersing effect upon the individual community in this way: If I belong to the community and I see advertised a car from Detroit, or milk produced by a national dairy conglomerate, or food shipped from some other part of the country, I will tend to buy these things. So my money goes out of the community.

My educational system trains me not for community life, but for service in industry, business, and cities—which again takes me out of the community. When I want to invest money my mind tends to go to the stock market, which is in New York or San Francisco; I invest in large national and international corporations, and my money goes out from the community. Also, jobs go out and away from the community. So there is this flow of finance and people out of the community, and when the community looks upon its own needs and attempts to do something about them, it does not have the resources, because very little flows back. If this trend continues, it would mean the destruction of small communities as viable economic and social units.

Morgan proposed a number of solutions to this. All of them in a way mirror the soul's attempt and need to individualise. They are all saying: There must be attention given to the immediate environment, to the small economic unit, whether it is the individual, the household, or the community—and this must be built before you attempt to expand to a national level of exchange.

He drew from history the example of a period from the 12th to the 15th century when there was no unemployment in Europe. There was no inflation and no recession largely because of the way currency was handled, which was quite different from the way we use currency today. We use our money, this manifestation, not only as a medium of exchange but also as a medium of saving. And most of us want to save, which is being into the process of involution, accumulation and focus. I am not saying this is wrong. I am only saying that we are working with *part* of the energy that is at our disposal. So we save this, and it goes out of circulation.

In the Middle Ages, during the time of the great guild system, money that was saved was taxed, so that it paid to keep money in circulation. Such a proposal was made in the United States Congress, to set up a system whereby all forms of saving were taxed, which would make it impractical for people to use money to save with. Of course, then they find other things to use as savings; and in the Middle Ages they used land. It was the hoarding of land that helped build up the feudal system. So everything has its pros and cons.

During the depression, however, there were small communities in the U.S. where the bankers instituted this system. They simply did not allow people to save money in their banks, but put the money back into circulation *within* the community. One way this was done was for the community to print its own money and charge a differential in which it was cheaper to use the community's money than to use the national money. For example, 10 national pounds would buy 11 community pounds, and it would be more expensive to go from community pounds back into national pounds.

The tendency, then, is to keep money in forms that can only be used within the community, and to finance and invest in community projects, which build up the economic base, provide employment, and develop the community as the economic focus. When the community is strong, it engages in financial interaction with the larger social structure as a whole unit.

In the United States—and it is probably true in Britain too—there is an economic unit which is more powerful, uses more money, and has more capital than all of the corporations put together. If you lump together General Motors, IBM, ITT and all their resources, there is still one other economic unit which is more powerful: the American household. In the U.S. there is a developing movement—in fact there's a book on it called *Home, Inc.*—to turn the attention of people back to the realisation of the amount of capital, investment and economic power that exists in the average household.

At the moment many households do not recognise themselves as a functioning individual unit. They surrender to the process of universalisation without the balance of the individual focus. So we have things done for us. We go out to the plumber, the doctor, the professional, when not so very long ago the average household did many things for itself. It made much of its own clothing, much of its own food. The father and mother took care of many of the medical chores for which we now would go to a doctor.

Throughout our society we see this movement of giving energy out to some larger unit, without the equal, balanced inflow to maintain the individual units. Often, the consequence is that the individual units begin to feel starved and become frantic. The reaction is not towards a balanced individuality, but towards an imbalanced individuality of further greed, further desire—a sense of "I must compete and get what I need because I have to resist all these forces that are taking everything from me and concentrating it in centres of power."

I am overdramatising this, but I want you to think of economics not only in terms of finance, buying and selling, goods and services, but to think of economics as energy flow, and to think of yourself, your family, your community and your nation each as an energy system. And I want you to consider how these energy systems interrelate creatively.

In the U.S. and Canada, a culture has been created that is very little in touch with the land. An overwhelming percentage of the population lives in cities. Now I feel this is a good thing, in one sense, because part of the challenge of human consciousness is to learn to see itself apart from its world, so that it can then more skilfully and consciously integrate with its world. There is an experiment in human consciousness going on as part of our evolutionary process. Part of what we're calling the new age is the evaluation of this experiment and its transition into a new way of relating the fruits of that experiment back to the Earth.

An example of this would be the New Alchemists, a group in Massachusetts, Canada and South America developing small technology systems which enable an average family to become completely self-sufficient on a very small amount of land. One of the exciting things about the New Alchemists, when they opened their experimental Bio-shelter on Prince Edward Island off the east coast of Canada, which is a building run entirely by solar energy and wind power, was that they not only generated sufficient electricity for their own needs but fed electricity back into the power grid of the island.

The vision of the New Alchemists is homes which generate their own power, their own food, and generate a surplus so that you have the household generating electricity which it can sell to the community—and whole neighbourhoods of households generating the electricity which the community requires.

To run a New Alchemist project requires a return to the consciousness of attunement to nature, but a different kind of consciousness than the traditional farmer would have—it is a more ecologically-minded, a more scientific consciousness in which the individual should see himself not just as a farmer but as part of an eco-system.

To return to our main points: There is a culture developing in North America which is distinct from the land on which it is surviving. I feel this has profound meanings, both positive and negative, in terms of what is being explored on the level of the human spirit. Economically, we see this in the development of large international corporations, or in a corporation in general, because a corporation is not a land-based entity, it is an abstraction. Where are General Motors, ITT, Philips, British Petroleum? They have their headquarters in different cities. They have their factories, their places of work and production. But the corporation itself does not exist in the same sense that San Francisco, London or Findhorn exists. It is not a place; it is an entity, an abstraction with great power, and an abstraction which is, to a considerable degree, divorced from the planet on which it is functioning. This has both positive and negative ramifications.

We are looking at the flow of the spirit to transform our society, looking at the continuous process by which our souls are learning to externalise more balanced, focused and whole human beings, but also learning to move with the process of planetary development, which requires the development of group consciousness, which requires the development of consciousnesses which span the planet.

For example, what is the community of Findhorn now? Is it just the people living here? There are hundreds of people in the United States now who have been at Findhorn for varying lengths of time. Many of these people feel deeply dedicated to this centre and part of it. If we think of Findhorn as having a consciousness, surely it includes these individuals as well. And surely the needs of the planetary crises that confront us, especially on the economic level, demand an ability to think of ourselves as part of the human species, not just as human beings confined to a particular geographic point.

The process of viewing the planet just as a resource must be reversed, causing us to focus on new ways to deal with the economic disparity of distribution and the need for sharing of resources on a planetary level. This focus must go all the way back down to the individual, to the nourishment of small units which can carry this focus into a new reality. How can a multi-national corporation embody the wholeness of the planet? How can a city, community or family embody this wholeness? How can you and I embody it and not lose our individuality in the process? How can we learn to spend 'planetary money' and not devalue our own currency, the currency of our own being?

On every level I feel this problem of balancing the energies of individualisation and universalisation is one way of describing this transitional period. It requires us to look at these processes. Do we want corporations to become simply vehicles through which we express or project our individual economic self? That is, is the corporation simply a way of making money for us? Or can we begin seeing corporations as ways of serving the planet—strategies for establishing planetary consciousness? What would this do to a corporation? Can there continue to be individual ownership of corporations? Or should corporations become communities in their own right owned by 'place' communities like Findhorn, Auroville, San Francisco, or conglomerates of people who use the corporation as a means of extending their own corporate economic power once they have established it within the well-being of their own community?

In the United States we see this struggle going on between greater governmental centralisation and decentralisation through states' power. Where does this power lie and how do we express it? Am I the source of power? Is my community? These are questions I feel we need to look at again, in the light of seeing ourselves as a strategy in planetary and human evolution moving in two directions at once—the deepening of our individual power to be a creative energy resource, and our communal power to blend and synthesise these resources in the creation of group wholeness.

My soul is not a consumer. My soul is a generator of energy. My personality, however, may think of itself as a consumer. The New Alchemist model reverses this and says: The home is not just a consumer, it is the economic unit of production. It produces the electricity, the food, the wherewithal of life. So we have this power, this generation of energy moving from the individual unit to the family unit to the collective group unit and so on out; an arising of energy, a release of that which has been involuted and accumulated, as opposed to looking out to some larger entity to supply our needs, whether that larger entity is God, the nation, the multinational corporation, or what is fed to us by advertising and other means of causing our consciousness to move away from the centre and to the periphery.

To study economics, to me, is to study the processes by which we become both individualised and harmonised with our environment. How do I become myself? How do I focus and take what I need to maintain myself in existence? How do I then become a generating, producing entity who can share freedom and courage with my world?

The study of economics is the study of energy flow, and so is the study of spiritual laws. In looking at economics we are looking at basic processes of soul and form, relationships between universal energy and crystallised energy. This makes the study of economics and the continual resolution of our economic problems truly a yoga for the human consciousness: a yoga of understanding what it means to be both an incarnating, finite entity and a divine, infinite entity at once.

I would like to elaborate on the fact that during the American Depression certain communities printed their own currency and established an exchange rate between their currency and the national currency. Under this exchange rate, for example, ten American dollars can buy eleven community dollars, so it is more profitable to exchange American money into community money than take money out of the community and put it into the larger national network. This makes me stop and think about where I want my energy to go, what I am trying to build. We are talking about creating semi-permeable membranes. All organisms have membranes that control and regulate the flow of energy between themselves and the environment. These membranes neither block that flow nor allow it to be unrestricted; if they did, life on a cellular level would cease: on the one hand the cell is ruptured, everything flows out and that's it, or, if it is too restricted, death occurs through lack of nourishment.

Economically, that kind of cell wall could be built around a community, encouraging the members to invest in community means of production and community services. If the community cannot provide certain services, it must either find ways in which it can develop the means of meeting them, or reach out to participate in the larger national network. But it must not look for everything from the national network.

I am now going to fantasise with you. I believe, in the new age, that this question of identity is going to be seen more in terms of creating semi-permeable membranes, which allow both creative, harmonious interaction between us and a creative, focused space within us, so that I have an individuality that is fluid in a very loving and wise way. These membranes will develop around cultural and geographical boundaries, what could be called the natural energy flows and patterns of humanity and of Earth. An example of this is that Africa was divided up into large tribal units. When the colonial powers took over and arbitrarily drew their boundaries, many of these boundaries cut through the tribal units, so you had a tribe existing in two countries. This has created considerable problems in Africa now.

The Earth is divided into its own kind of organic geography, where, for example, the energy of Scotland is different from the energy of England, which is different from the energy of Wales. These are *not* the same place, even though they are the same island. Is it possible, with sensitivity and insight, to perceive what these differences are and work to nourish Scotland, Wales or England—and out of that larger nourishment create membranes which then link into a larger organism which is the individuality of the British Isles?

Although I don't think they have much chance at the moment, there are, in fact, some plans in the United States for breaking down the nation into smaller, more manageable units based on geography, culture, language, productive capacities—in short, the identity of a region, which is whole in itself. Out of that wholeness the region can blend with other regions. Perhaps the multinational corporations, which transcend nation-states, may be some of the evolving structures that can help bring this about. I do not know. It depends on how these structures evolve and how we help to evolve them.

Chapter Seven
THE POLITICS OF MYSTICISM

WE ARE now entering a time of great outpouring of spiritual energy, of life, of light into the spheres of human consciousness. This is having an effect and is going to have an increasing effect on the patterns of human behaviour, human culture, and indeed on all that proceeds from that creative centre which we call the human race.

Since we are given an opportunity to share with the Divine this remarkable adventure of helping to build a new world, of helping to create a new heaven and a new Earth, of being not just the instruments through which the divine plan is manifested but the livingness of the plan itself, it is good that we can have an understanding and a vision of all that is emerging for us so that we can be better architects of Aquarius.

Ages ago when the Atlantean civilisation was strong and its influence radiating out into the world, people dwelt in a consciousness which was far more oriented to the emotional body and to astral awareness than is the case now. Humanity was largely clairvoyant—sensitive to the super-sensible realms, or at least to some of them—and ordered its life and conducted its culture along lines that would seem quite strange to us today.

The human race at that time was a child, an infant in many spiritual ways. As a consequence it was watched over, guided and guarded by beings of considerable wisdom, light and stature, who quite literally enfolded the environment of humanity's mental and emotional worlds with the energies which they wished humanity to absorb—in much the same way that good gardeners today place into the soil the nourishment they wish the plants to absorb so that they may grow the better.

In those days, humanity was very responsive to this kind of treatment. It functioned with a far more instinctive consciousness, a consciousness of the group—a group which was not composed of independent individuals but of linked individuals who were responding *en masse* to various patterns of thought.

It was out of that environment and within that context that there arose the traditions of the priest-king and of the spiritual leader who was quite literally the spiritual father for his people. He provided the focus through his consciousness, the framework through his mind and heart, for the release of that structure of energy within which his people could evolve. He was their shepherd, their guide, their protector and their authority. On many levels he was their king. When this individual was himself attuned and part of the evolutionary brotherhood of light, all went well. In the early days of human history this was almost always the case.

As humanity began to grow and tap the sources of energy within itself, however, it also discovered that it had a remarkable ability to isolate itself from the streams of behaviour, impression and instinct which were modifying the behaviour of its fellows. The individual discovered, in fact, that one could exist and function as an individual self, and that the key to this existence and functioning lay within an exciting new realm which was the mental realm, the mind, the ability to reason for one's self. As people began to develop their mental capacities, as indeed they had to, and increasingly were placed into positions of having to make choices and evaluate circumstances in ways that would cause their minds to grow, the pattern of free will became much more evident within human experience. Out of this emerged those individuals who could say with perfect freedom from that which was flowing about them, "No, this is not the course that I wish to take. Rather I will go along this route."

Many times this was a good action. At the same time there developed those individuals who discovered that their own independence and developing selfhood could be a tool in their hands to influence great numbers of people. Out of this arose the tradition of the left hand path, the brothers of darkness, who are essentially and primarily beings who channel energy for the manipulation of their own environment to their own ends.* These are beings who have failed to recognise the infinite splendour that is within them. They have failed to recognise that they are one with the whole. Through this failure, through seeing themselves as separate, what was born within their consciousnesses was a need to protect that separateness and to make of it a source and centre of power,

*See 'Rhythms of Evolution' in *Reflections on the Christ* (Findhorn Publications)

so that whatever they needed—whether it be wealth or influence or people—could be attracted and held. As this developed it eventually led to the destruction of the Atlantean civilisation, as those who were seeking to guard the race came into conflict with those who were seeking to manipulate it.

The time in which we are living is a repeat of the Atlantean experience on a higher level of the spiral. Humanity's psychic faculties were turned off to protect it in those days, and in that way a great deal of the power of those who would manipulate was also cut off. Humanity was launched into developing its rational faculties. The principle of rulership by the few—and in many cases by the one, the monarch—continued, but now increasingly began moving onto a personality level. This meant rulership through power, through authority, rather than rulership through vision.

This was not only true in the sphere of temporal power but also in the sphere of sacred power. It became necessary in these ancient times for those who were the guardians of the mysteries to be powerful centres of authority in order to ensure that purity was maintained. The spiritual teacher, the hierophant, the guru, demanded obedience—they demanded that one turn oneself over to their consciousnesses so that they knew with absolute reliance that the energies for which they were the transmitting point would be used properly.

As humanity continued to develop, and more and more people experienced the awareness of self, this pattern had to break. Its breaking point—both in occultism and esoteric thought—came within the Western tradition through the development of scientific thought, of rationalism and all that followed in terms of technology.

It is interesting that one of the major foundations for the new age unfoldment developed during that time when rational scepticism came into being and was fostered throughout the European culture. The guardians of the race foresaw the time in which we are now living, and recognised the powers that would be invoked—the powers that individuals can draw to themselves from many higher realms which make them charismatic centres of influence. They realised that the etheric veil surrounding the planet, the so-called veil of the temple which has protected humanity from many influences from outside, would be rent. Through these holes would come energies, visions and awareness,

66

much of which would be good but a lot of which would be basically illusion. Some would also be offsprings of ancient forms of manipulation dressed up in modern usage.

To protect the race against this, a healthy and necessary consciousness of materialistic scepticism was introduced into the mass consciousness. The materialism from which we are now struggling has been in many cases the guardian of the race for the past three hundred years or so. It continues to be to this day.

We need to understand why this is so. Jesus said, when asked what the last days would be like, the days before the return or the reappearance of the Christ-consciousness upon the Earth, that many would come forward claiming to be the Christ. People would say "Lo he is here, lo he is there," and many would be deceived, for reasons which I will enter into later. But many will not be deceived, simply because their consciousness is fixed with a certain kind of materialistic bent that does not open them readily to the vision and the energies of the higher realms, or indeed to anything of a so-called mystical or spiritual nature, until a sufficient structure of discrimination and wisdom exists upon the Earth, whose purity ensures that that which is trans-mitted into the human consciousness is also pure. The person who has a sceptical attitude towards the return of the Christ, for example, is not in general one who is likely to get caught up in "Lo he is here, lo he is there," and the confusion that follows.

I mention this simply because I wish you to understand that throughout history *all* movements in human consciousness have served and are serving a divine purpose. We are struggling with materialism at this point because it has served its purpose, and we are now reaching for a greater purity, a greater light; but that same consciousness of scepticism and scientific rationality has served and is serving still as a guardian of racial awareness.

We are in an interim age. We are in an age when many forces are being brought into conflict, and in the dust that is raised through this conflict there is much confusion upon the Earth. Humanity is still close enough to its infancy, its adolescence as a race, to fear the unknown, to fear confusion and to fear the insecurity which it brings. Humanity has only recently experienced democracy—which is one of the great revelations brought to human consciousness—to learn that an evolutionary force can emerge from the mass of human consciousness rather than from a few individual points. It has been my personal experience that there are people who, though very happy intellectually that they live in a democracy, are not particularly happy about it emotionally or even spiritually. From the depths of the race a call is rising for the emergence of a saviour, an avatar, a father-figure, a being, a personage who can be for the race what the ancient priest-kings were in the dawn of human history.

This is having a very interesting effect upon the inner realms. It is drawing forward atavistic or primeval thought-forms born out of the Atlantean time. Individuals, groups and images are emerging, almost pulled into existence by the demand of people, to be unto those people saviours, guides and organising structures.

If we examine the classical mystical tradition in the West and East, we find that it is hierarchical in nature. It is based upon a system of relative evolutionary status. I am more evolved than you, or he is more evolved than me, and so on. This is an ideal system for consciousnesses that require external support and strength to help them be what they essentially are anyway. It has been suggested of course that much of the resurgence of mysticism and occultism within the West at the present time—the entering into the West of patterns of Eastern occultism, yoga, and many gurus that are travelling throughout the world—is to bring about a blend of Eastern and Western culture, and of spiritual values which will awaken the West from its materialism. I am quite sure this is happening and this is quite right. At the same time, however, the West is faced with the challenge of its society seeking some kind of power structure, or some kind of being, upon which it can place faith, dependency and allegiance in order to help it through what it conceives to be the morass of the present state. This is in fact invoking a return into the West of very ancient patterns. It is invoking the guru, invoking the master; it is invoking that which will be to the Western mind a saviour which may help the West get rid of this awful burden of the mind.

People are quite happily throwing discrimination to the winds and relying upon their emotionalism to guide them to people whom they feel will represent for them the source of help and support. This is retrograde because it is operating on the Atlantean level without carrying it to a higher level of the spiral.

For centuries humanity has been evolving its mentality so that it might be the bridge to its intuition, that it might be the great guardian to help people discriminate between what is emotionalism—in terms of "I feel this is right"and "I feel this is good"—and true intuition, which is pure identification with truth. The human race has been developing a certain basic wisdom and common sense which can serve it now if it will give it half a chance.

Many occult schools are teaching that we are now in the time of the externalisation of the hierarchy, that band of highly evolved beings who have been the guardians of the race throughout history. I for one believe that this is so. Yet I would like to suggest that this concept has suffered in much the same way that many concepts of spiritual truth have because we are seeing them through the prism of past conditioning and past needs. We see the hierarchy as a group of individuals of high evolutionary status without fully perceiving that what we are dealing with when we consider the hierarchy is a natural force. There is quite a difference between an organic hierarchy and an organisational one which is created by the human mind or mental perception.

What is this difference? If you are in a family and you have brothers and sisters, then your older brother may be in one sense ahead of you and have certain rights within the family—he gets to choose what television shows he is going to watch because he is older. But we generally do not think of the older brother as being in a hierarchical position. He is within the organisation of the family; through his further experience and wider knowledge he is a being who has the potential to enhance your growth. He can help to create and provide the environment of wisdom, light, nourishment and love within which you can unfold.

I may be describing an ideal family, but that is the way the spiritual hierarchy works. They are not organisational beings as much as they are beings who have so identified themselves with certain natural energies that they become the conduits through which these energies may enter human experience.

The hierarchy has its exact counterpart within ourselves, however. The Christ has his counterpart within me—the Christ within. The Lord of Civilisation has his counterpart within me: the civilising consciousness within my own being. The purpose of the hierarchy is to reflect to us the reality that is within *so that we become that reality*. It is prophesied by the hierarchy itself that the time will come when it will cease to exist because it will have absorbed completely into humanity, and humanity will actually *be* the hierarchy. It will be the illumined collective consciousness.

In dealing with this externalisation of the hierarchy, and viewing the fact that within modern culture there is this yearning for someone or something that can tell us how to save ourselves—and there are plenty of people who are willing to step into that position—it is important that we raise our vision so as not to allow the energies to express themselves in that fashion. Otherwise what we will externalise is certainly a hierarchy, but one that is a throw-back to the kingly, priestly hierarchies of the past, and one which is not in progression with the divine impulse of democracy anchored—relatively speaking—a short time ago.

What would be a theocratic democracy? That is what we are trying to evolve at Findhorn. It is a state in which each individual is engaged in a continual process of depth-understanding, self-transformation, self-attunement, and the generating of that inner consciousness that places the individual at one with the Divine, not only as an external reality but also as that which is emerging from within one's self.

For this eventually to come about requires individuals who have learned how to purify themselves, how to communicate with others and how to create a group consciousness. Those are the primary tasks before us in helping to externalise the true hierarchy, the true organic unfoldment of a oneness-consciousness. The mind must be transcended but not eliminated. If it is not transcended, our hierarchies become structural and limiting. If it is transcended into mindlessness and eliminated, then we are wide open to the same kind of control and influence which is so potential today through all that is unfolding.

The Atlantean adepts were somewhat limited in the range to which they could project their influence. Today's adepts, whoever they may be, are not limited, because they have before them the tremendous outreach or capacity of the media. The problem is that people are rapidly becoming conditioned through our educational process to believe what they are told through the media. If it is in print, it must be true. If someone says it over television or radio then it carries a certain impact.

So this is how we begin, if we are to allow the new mystical consciousness to unfold and not fall into either of the patterns of the past—the manipulative hierarchical pattern or the kind of democratic pattern which is based on majority rule and quantity-consciousness and power rather than on vision and consciousness of quality. Democracy by majority rule is often misdirected by the power of the lowest common denominator. It has always been a few individuals at the crest of the wave—the creative minority—who have moved forward and externalised the new vision.

Purity is the first step—individual purity and purity of awareness. This means that I, as an individual, must be aware of myself and aware of my world sufficiently to know where I stand in relationship to other people. I must know, for example, where my needs and power-hangups may lie, if I have them.

It means that if I receive energy from the higher realms (as indeed I may, because most people are going to be receiving it in one form or another, and we are all asked at this time to claim our Christhood and to begin to act as spiritual beings for the race) then that which I receive should integrate me and come within the purview of an illumined mind, an illumined heart and a stable body structure.

This purity is a state in which synthesis has been achieved. It is the purity of selfless service in which we recognise, as Jesus said, that he who would be greatest must be the least. The mark of the true soul-consciousness and of the true disciple is a willingness to serve with joy and with love in whatever capacity that person is asked to serve. It is a willingness to be at peace and at rest internally so that the dynamics of action can flow through one, not necessarily from one.

It means that it is not my personality that is generating all the activity that surrounds me, but it is the will of the world. It is my sensitivity through love and wisdom to what is needed and my relationship to that need that generates what comes through me. It is not just looking out and saying, "Well, I feel I should do this; this is the best plan," but to be still enough that I can truly hear the voice of the spirit in that moment. That is the living Plan.

This purity also implies discipline. It implies that the mind is used with awareness, with a reasonable common sense, a certain balanced scepticism coupled with true openness—a willingness to listen and observe before jumping to conclusions. It is an ability to accept the identity of the divine in myself without being afraid of it.

There are many people now who are facing the crisis of messiahship simply because it is time for the arising of the peoples of the Earth to do that which Jesus demonstrated. What do I do when the finger of God is laid upon me and he says, "Will you take me as yourself and be my life?" Can I look upon myself and my task within the world with sufficient perspective and balance and yet sufficient love and awareness that I can accept that and go forth as a divine being? That is a new kind of purity. It is a challenging one. It requires a great deal of courage—not courage in the face of danger but the courage to trust oneself—and at the same time discrimination, so that I am aware of where my current limitations lie and do not become distorted by them.

In the past, the guru has been the one who through his own force of consciousness and attunement has been able to take on the auric fields, the energies, the patterns of his disciples, and lift them in some way (although that has been more true of the Eastern pattern than of the West; Western occultism has almost always demanded a larger degree of individual self-government and responsibility). Now, however, a new pattern is seeking emergence. It is a little difficult to see in our present world, because what is apparent on the surface is a lot of new gurus popping up all over the place. What is seeking to emerge is a body of people who are nourishers and who are quite literally what Jesus called 'the salt of the Earth', but consciously so, spiritually so, accepting their divinity without becoming inflated by it, and acting within the sphere of their influence to draw that same divinity out of others.

These are givers of life, and they are forming the basis for the government of the future. This will be a government that is authoritarian, but authoritarian in the same way that the laws of thermodynamics or of gravity are authoritarian. The radiance and vibration of attunement with the Beloved, the sense of being at one with the currents of life, become so strong that a person recognises, "If I really want to be what I am, then I cannot do this, I cannot do the other thing. I can only follow this rhythm, this pattern."

It is a form of self-government, but it is also government by the whole, the true democracy: a 'holocracy', holistic consciousness made manifest.

It is important to understand that this is the way the hierarchy functions. In essence, the hierarchy is a single being, and that is often the way in which the hierarchy is contacted. You may come in contact with a particular master but he only represents a single group consciousness. It is difficult for human beings, still caught on the level of identification with fragmentary and personality forms, to recognise that they are dealing with a group consciousness which is still a single consciousness. New age unfoldment is not going to be brought about by leadership. It cannot be. It is not going to be brought about by the appearance upon the Earth of a whole new race of super-beings who will take humanity by the hand and say, "This is the way to go." It is being brought about by a concerted effort on the part of the forces of light to inspire humanity towards its maturity and divinity.

I see this as a problem of education, but we cannot wait for the great ones to appear and educate us. It is a cooperative venture, such as we find in many free universities where student and teacher roles tend to merge and the two help to plan the curriculum. It is like saying, "All right. If I know what the vision is, if I know that the divine pattern now is to make of me a self-governing being, one with the rhythms of life, one with the whole, then what can I do to promote that? If I enter an organisation, if I become part of a community, what can I do to make that community, that organisation more of a unity, of a wholeness? What can I do to dissipate or dissolve inappropriate boundaries and distribute the forces of awareness and of authority? What can I do to be an authority? What can I do to shoulder my share of responsibility for the whole?"

When you come into the presence of someone who is more knowledgeable in a certain area, you are often very aware of it, and, if you have any sense at all, you are willing to give to that person authority for that area, sapiential authority, authority through greater knowledge or awareness. For example, if I wanted to learn to work in the garden and placed myself under an expert's guruship, it would be silly for me to say, "My consciousness tells me that this heather plant should be cut this way," when my teacher is someone who knows how a plant should be cut. At that point the teacher is a representative of the consciousness of the plant and it would be a joy and only right to place myself within my teacher's authority. That is the action of holocracy: to give authority willingly to another whom we recognise as having that authority in certain areas, but to keep it for ourselves in those areas where we recognise that we have it. Ultimately we are the authority for how good a job we do, or how much purity and love and awareness we put into it.

What I feel many spiritual teachers are not recognising at this point—because instead they recognise a need on the part of humanity and are trying to answer that—is that they are, in trying to answer the need, throwing the true answer out and substituting a temporary one. Let us be aware that we cannot, if we want to build a new age, simply meet a symptom of humanity's present need. People need leadership, spiritual leadership. Many sensitive people feel this, and they are capable of meeting it and will move to meet it. At the same time, however, as we become aware of this and as each of us does seek to meet it, let us be aware that we cannot meet it simply by fulfilling a person's need for a guru and by standing on mystical authority. We meet it by standing on the authority of what we are and by demonstrating what we are to that person, if we can respond to the deeper need of that person, which is to be free, which is to know the divinity of himself or herself and to be given the priceless gift of being a truly free agent.

People talk about having free will, but they have not had any free will for centuries. They never bother to exercise it. Most people's choices which are called 'free will' are dictated by other forces—by manifestations of fear, mass thought, conditioning, and value systems which are socially acceptable.

If we can give people the ability of independent awareness and thought, then we are giving them a priceless gift if at the same time that independent awareness and thought is at one with the presence of the Beloved within, the wholeness. That is the greatest freedom.

God acts with no limitation. His action is joy, and such limitation as he does accept willingly is to enhance that joy, with the limitations which we call natural laws.

Findhorn has often been criticised because it is not meeting the apparent needs of the world. It is not going out and generating food for starving people. It is not going out and ministering to drug-crazed young people in the slums. It is not going out and ministering to the sick and needy. Once, when Jesus was eating, Mary Magdalene came in with a jar of precious ointment and sought to anoint him with it. Judas stood up and said, "Woman, you could sell this and give the money to the poor," and Jesus said, "The poor are always with you and I am not." The need of humanity is always there until we get down to certain root causes and eliminate them.

In meeting the need of the world, this crying out of humanity for something which will lead it—for a structure that it can hold onto during this time of tremendous change—can invoke either a very powerful political structure, a conservative structure, a dictatorship or a totalitarian state, or it can invoke the same thing coming from the spiritual side, *if* what we are trying to do is meet the need of the people.

On the other hand, we can meet the reality of our own identity and translate that identity of oneness with the whole out into the world, saying, "I am the Beloved, I am the Divine, I am one with God, I can dispense light, love, compassion, wisdom, through whatever I am doing. If I am woodworking, I can love that wood. If I am gardening, I can love what I am doing." That whole sense of joy and participation in the communion of building the Earth is infectious and spreads to others and awakens within them the fact that we are creators. We are not the victims of this life, we are creators within it.

Then we are helping to invoke a new form of government, a government of purity of motive, purity of awareness, a government of the soul rather than of the personality. Even if the personality motives are of the highest, they tend to produce tunnel vision and to meet the needs of other personalities. Because I, as a personality, would suffer if I were hungry or poor, so I can recognise that need and will seek to meet it specifically. But the soul will go directly to meet a deeper need, which on a causal, creative level is creating the hunger and poverty in the first place.

We are seeking to create a holocracy which emerges through a pure sensitivity to what is right in the moment, what is the living plan in the moment, not as an external authority but as an emergent creative activity. It requires as the first step that we begin to recognise that the revelation of our age is not a whole new mystical revival movement like so many such movements that are spreading across the land, but is a recognition that God is offering to us a partnership in building a new world, and that the creative power for that, the vision for it, the life for it, exists within ourselves.

We can begin to look at ourselves honestly. We can accept our hangups. We can accept our areas of failure and areas of challenge, but at the same time accept the divinity that is there, too, and not be frightened by what it asks of us. The painting 'The Light of the World' by Holman Hunt shows Jesus knocking on a door. The

Christ, the light, knocks on the door of human consciousness, and people within say, "All right, I'm coming, but first let me determine where the chinks in my armour are, the cracks in the wall." We look at our household: we see the dust on the mantle; we see the dishes that have not been washed; we see the bed that has not been made. We see all the things in this house that we really would not want the Christ to see if we let him in. So we say, "Just a minute, wait until I clean things up," without realising that He has come to help us clean. He comes to give us the sense of identity which is resurrecting and to purify that ego, that aspect of ourselves which we reject, the dweller on the threshold, that whole portion of human consciousness in which we say, "That's not of me, I don't want to be part of that."

Within that lies our hunger for power because we create our own impotency. We create our sense of powerlessness and therefore we seek those with whom we can identify who seem to us powerful. We seek a group, a teacher, a teaching, with which we can identify—just as the ancient tribes had their totems, or Japanese workers get up every morning and sing the company song in unison, or people cluster together with various kinds of artificial aids to communal togetherness. Let us all dance together, and let us have slogans together and let us have badges. We seek to answer a deep feeling of powerlessness in the face of an unknown universe. But we are not willing to take the basic steps of accepting the divine power, the love, the trust that is within us that can answer this.

It is that step and that alone which will solve the problem of our future political system and enable us to invoke the true system that is attempting to unfold—a system in which it is not one person who is dictating what must be done. It is not the Christ as the head of the heirarchy who says, "All right, this is what must be done." It is that which is emergent as the divine spirit within humanity, within the nature kingdom, within all kingdoms which says, "I am the plan, I am the goal, I am the dream. Help me to unfold. Give me birth." And the Christ says, "I am your servant, I am your Beloved and I will help you unfold." It is not one person saying, "This is what you will learn, this is how you will do it." It is one person saying, "That which is there within you is struggling to emerge, and how fantastically beautiful it is, how joyous it is that with my skill or with my knowledge or with my whatever I have, no matter how humble or how skilful it may be, I can help it emerge." This is the aristrocracy of the servant consciousness of the soul.

Mysticism and the mystics are seen as that pattern in human consciousness and those people who have access to realms denied to ordinary people. There is certainly a good deal of glamour that surrounds this. The witch-doctor, the priest, the shaman, all of them were surrounded by a certain aura of being in contact with that which the ordinary person is not in contact with.

But the message that the new age seeks to give is that there is no such thing as an ordinary person, any more than there is any such thing as an ordinary God. We are each in contact with this divinity; and in a world in which we are asked to bring heaven down and externalise it, quite often the gardener, the carpenter, the mechanic, the person who can work with hands, with mind, with heart, the scientist, the technician, the individual who can actually create the beauty in form, is being far more mystical and spiritual than the person who simply goes to other realms and communicates back to people what is there.

The heirarchy of the future is a hierarchy of service and of mutual sharing of what we are, so that we can build this world, and recognise (as Teilhard de Chardin puts it so well) that the mystical consciousness is the basic consciousness for humanity. A person who, in creating a pot or a rack for things to hang on, or furniture or whatever, can blend with that project, can love it, and can see the divine within it, is in a mystical state, the same as the person who is floating about some place in meditation.

On the other hand, the person in meditation who can bring through vision and awareness and energy from other realms also adds to the whole. Every bit of it is required as long as we maintain our perspectives and do not allow ourselves to fall again into the various well-defined roles of teacher-student, guru-chela, and so on.

The politics of mysticism, then, arise when each can perceive that they are mystic. They are a child of God. They *are* the authority, not in conflict with others, not in demanding an ego-right to have the last say and to hold sway over others, but to the extent that the voice of the whole which is their true voice can speak through them and that the heart and mind of the Beloved can find within them the means to embrace creation—and with the fire of that passionate embrace lift it to the heights and reveal its splendour.

Chapter Eight
THE POLITICS OF SYNERGY

IN THE last chapter we traced the relationship of humanity to those energies which in the past have represented its source of direction: energies of wisdom, of intelligence, of power, of will, of spirit, usually embodied in some priestly figure or king.

As people evolved and increasingly discovered the secrets and powers of their own selves, they wanted to exercise this capacity of self through their own style of individual leadership. The whole pattern of leadership, of group work, of politics, began to shift increasingly toward personality levels of expression until in the days of Atlantis the final climax came and humanity made a great leap into a new cycle of being, but one which in many ways represented a plunge into greater density than it had previously known.

Our own age is in some ways a repetition on a much higher level of the evolutionary cycle of the days of Atlantis, when humanity first began to confront the challenge of self and to discover within this challenge new sources of personal and group power. Now humanity is undergoing another vast evolutionary change which is symbolised both factually and allegorically by the concept of a new age, the Age of Aquarius.

There is great confusion in any period of transition. Old values and institutions are falling away, new ones have not yet clarified themselves sufficiently to take their place. People feel insecure and caught in the shifting of the world they have known. It is like a psychic, spiritual, intellectual, emotional earthquake. During such a period there is a natural tendency to seek out points of stability, and in the field of politics and psychological need such points of stability are generally strong individuals: individuals who have clear vision, who have a sense of destiny, of power, who know where they are going and who can inspire in others a sense of stability.

For this reason we are in a time similar to what Jesus foretold, when people would look to find the energies of the Christ and of spiritual leadership and would find it here and there and almost everywhere that they looked, until even those who had the greatest discrimination would face the test of being caught in the illusion of this search. This is the greatest challenge facing us now: how to move through this age and evolve a new form of politics without becoming caught in our needs and desires for the kind of stability which appears useful but which in truth is retrogressive.

Piscean leadership, that is, the leadership of the old age, the one that is disappearing, may be characterised as hierarchical in form: one person at the summit of power who dispenses this power through others who are in lesser positions under him. It may be described as a sun-satellite system in which the strong individuals occupy the centre and others revolve around them and their particular power, whatever that power happens to be, whether it is financial, emotional, mental or spiritual. In our day there are many gurus, would-be masters, seeming avatars and others, who would meet this need in the human psyche but would meet it using old age methods, and set themselves up as if they were the embodiment of the great divine master who is within us each.

What is the new pattern that is unfolding, and how can we recognise it?

I call this new pattern the politics of synergy. Synergy is a word coined by an American anthropologist to describe a social state in which the whole is greater than the sum of its parts, and yet the whole is not in conflict with its parts; every individual who makes up that social system being blessed and fulfilled by it. Synergy is a state of being, a social state or an energy state in which the various component units all interact in such a way that no one unit wins out over the others and no one unit loses to the others. Everyone gains and, as a result, the whole that is the greater manifestation which they are forming is stronger, more efficient, better organised and more life-fulfilling than it would otherwise be.

An example of synergy would be a marriage in which both husband and wife blend together in such a way that both can grow in freedom, both are strengthened by the relationship, and can be and do more together than they could be and do if they were apart.

Synergy is closely related to the concept of synthesis, which is one of the key concepts underlying the new age.

Synergy also represents the future of group consciousness, and therefore I wish to suggest that the politics of the future will not revolve around individuals, powerful leaders, politicians, statesmen, religious figures, economists and so forth. It will revolve around the ability of individuals to pool their lives, their skills, their talents into a group endeavour and create a group consciousness. Perhaps in the future we shall elect groups to govern our societies and our states—groups that have demonstrated their attunement together and their ability to work together in a state of synergy. That, however, remains to be seen.

Let us explore this concept of the development of a synergic group consciousness. There are three key words that I would like to suggest. The first is custodianship, the second is sacrifice and the third is synthesis.

Most people view themselves as possessors. We own or possess the things that enter our life, the things that we purchase with the money that we have earned through our labours. I own my car, I own my house, I own this furniture or that book. The concept of ownership is deeply rooted in human consciousness, and as an experience formed an integral part of the evolutionary process of individualisation, the development of selfhood. People, individual people, identifying with property they own, extend their identity into these things. Their possessions help to identify them and they in turn identify their possessions through their own being. We say the house reflects the personality of the people who live in it. Likewise we say they are the people who live in that house, he is the man who owns that yacht, and so forth. The concept of ownership in human society has also extended to ownership over abstractions like ideas and over other living things: animals, plants and people.

It is in this area that humanity now needs to evolve a new way of looking at itself and its world. The new age is an exercise in re-identification. It is an exercise of humanity's learning to re-define what it is—as a result of which, because people learn to attune to the level of their souls, the level of their true inner causal identities, they do not need to own things in order to feel that they are 'a person'. They do not need to show possessions to the world in order to demonstrate identity. A person is what a person is. One can say "I am that I am," and not require any external aid to help in this act of identification.

Therefore, those persons are very free where possessions are concerned, and understand that everything that exists is part of one wholeness, just as they are part of that wholeness. Their relationship to the earth, to plants, to nature, to rivers and oceans, to the air, to animals and to other people is the kind of relationship that people have to members of their own family. All these elements of our environment, including ourselves, spring from a single source and that source is God.

When various elements come into our so-called ownership, the new consciousness views them as coming into a person's custodianship. I do not own this thing; I do not possess this money. I am its custodian. I am here to see that it is used in the best way possible. I am here to see that it fulfils its part in the whole, to help it to integrate, to help it circulate.

In the true consciousness of custodianship, there is no fear. Individuals can release that of which they have been custodians when they know that this release is the best way to fulfil duties: for example, the release of money to places where it is needed when we do not have need of it and knowing that our needs will be met when they arise; the release of tangible goods to places where they are needed; the release of those things which we have owned but which no longer serve any purpose for us; and most importantly where the politics of the new age are concerned, the release of people.

In many areas of human life and society it is all too common to find the concept of people owning people. It has distinguished the marriage contract for centuries, and likewise it has been part of humanity's group experience. How many times have we heard earnest and otherwise sincere group leaders speak about "my group, my people, my followers," and become upset when these individuals decide to leave the group or to leave that particular pattern of teaching or that particular teacher?

Every group comes into existence to be an evolutionary aid to the development and growth of the individuals that comprise it, just as the Earth has been brought into existence to assist the formless life of God to grow and expand through experience in form. Humanity has viewed its world as something to conquer and dominate, not as something of which it is the custodian. Now, however, with the crisis of pollution and the very real threat of human extinction, people are having to adjust their consciousnesses. They know they cannot treat rivers, oceans, air, plants and animals as if they were mere adjuncts to human will and human wishes, placed on earth simply to fulfil human desires. Humanity must be like the elder brother to the environment, to help it unfold the divine potentials already inherent within it.

Likewise in a group, the group leader is there to help unfold and reveal the divine potential inherent in the people who comprise the group. The leader does not own them, does not control them, does not manipulate them. The leader is there to serve, and to see that the potential is actualised and brought into manifestation.

Therefore this concept of custodianship is a key one, particularly where the politics of group development in the new age are concerned. In it and because of it every member of a group learns that they are the custodians of the well-being and development of every other member and works with that aim in mind, to serve the whole.

The second concept is the concept of **sacrifice**. Sacrifice is a very much misunderstood concept. Viewed from a form level and from a personality viewpoint it means giving up something, generally giving up something to which one has become attached, often possessions or people that we feel possessive of. If there were no sense of attachment, we would not regard such a release as a sacrifice. If you give something away for which you have no use and which means nothing to you, you generally do not think of it as a sacrifice; but to give up money or possessions which are meaningful to you or which you identify as being necessary to your well-being—that is a sacrifice.

So we see that the concept of custodianship is very much linked to the one of sacrifice. A person who has a true sense of being simply a custodian, working for the well-being of those people or elements which are brought within one's care, does not have a sense of sacrifice when the time comes to release them.

On a much higher level, sacrifice means something entirely different from giving up. It comes from the same root word as 'sacred' and 'sanctify', and it means 'to make holy'. From an occult viewpoint, sacrifice means the taking on of a new relationship, the taking on of a new identity. How is this possible? Sacrifice, true sacrifice, means that I identify myself with something beyond myself, such as a family, or another person, or a greater whole—mental, emotional, physical or spiritual—of which I may be a part. And because I take on the sense of greater perspective, and I identify myself with that greater whole, my own possessions or objects of custodianship are viewed in a different perspective as well.

Sacrifice, where group development is concerned, simply means that I come to realise that my true identity is the identity that moves through all the group. It is a greater self of love, of wisdom, of intelligence, of light, of will, which operates on such a high or fundamental level that everyone within the group partakes of it. It transcends our differences and our similarities. It transcends everything on a form level and makes us essentially united. When I identify with that or take on the mantle of that identification, then I will act in such a way as to care for and build up the nature and qualities of that identity. In other words I serve the whole.

In so doing I may have to forego certain personal patterns of action, of pleasure, of fulfilment which previously I had been free to pursue, but I do not miss them. They no longer represent pleasure or fulfilment to me. What represents pleasure and fulfilment arises from manifestations affecting the group wholeness and its well-being.

In ancient times, when a person was sacrificed to the gods it was considered a great honour, mainly because the sacrifice meant that that person was in a new relationship to the god. Individuals who were to be sacrificed were quite often looked upon as a god themselves. They had taken on a new identity. They had transcended themselves, translated their old selves and given them a new birth.

In modern times we do not sacrifice people in that way, at least not as objectively or as apparently. The concept of true sacrifice, however, is an important one to spiritual development and to the development of group consciousness. It means simply the taking on of a new relationship, the taking on of a new identity, the translation of the self into a greater perspective than it previously had. On the outer levels and to someone who does not perceive what is happening on the inner, it may appear that such a person is giving up various things or qualities, but to the person who is truly involved and who understands, no loss is experienced, only gain.

Out of this gain comes the third key word, which is **synthesis.** What is synthesis? We think of synthetics as that which is man-made and artificial; brought about, through the actions of intelligence, by combining various elements that would not otherwise be combined and creating from them something: a wholeness, a combination, an amalgamation that had not previously existed.

Synthesis means to bring together and to unite in that togetherness, generally in such a fashion that that which is created through that unity is greater than the sum of its individual parts.

Within a group, synthesis of consciousness does not mean the same thing as democracy. I feel this is very important to understand, for democracy as we generally express it in a political sense, on a form and personality level, means the rule of the majority. It says nothing about synthesis, nothing about the creation of a group consciousness, nothing about the ability of a group of people to commune together, to communicate together, and to evolve out of their communion that which is for the highest good of all. It simply says that the will of the greatest number will decide what must be done. In this sense democracy is a needed step in the development of group consciousness and is an important step away from the more ancient forms of monarchy and priestly rule which characterised the Atlantean dispensations of consciousness. But democracy practiced only on a form level does not represent the true politics of the new age.

We have an important clue in this term synthesis, for here we have a group of people coming together to blend themselves. They have a will to become one, not to find out what the majority thinks and to follow the majority but quite literally to go beyond their personal selves in an attempt to discover and to externalise a greater oneness, a greater self, a greater wholeness—in other words to create a state of synergy.

What emerges from such a group consciousness is a true unity of purpose and decision. It may be focused in one or two individuals within the group who become, as it were, facilitators or focalisers through which the group energy can move and focus itself to accomplish its purposes. A focaliser is one who like a lens gathers together the elements and enables synthesis to take place through the focusing of these elements into a unity. It is like a lens that gathers the energy of the sun and focuses it to create heat. The focaliser may be the individual or group of individuals or idea which acts as a synthesising point within the group; the energy or the centre which allows the whole to come together.

A leader in the old sense represents the one who tells others what to do, and in some fashion imposes one's will and direction upon the group. Out of true sacrifice, which is the taking on of a greater sense of identity, of identifying oneself with that inner self that is the source of our life and which itself is the souce of wholeness, a person is placed into a position of being able to accomplish synthesis with others—through love, through wisdom, through intelligence and through the will to good that on human levels manifests as goodwill.

It is important to understand that this kind of sacrifice and synthesis does not mean the loss of the individual. This is what happens in groups, organisations and nations operating under an old age consciousness, struggling to conceptualise and externalise the idea of the whole and serving the whole, but actually doing it through the sacrifice of the part in the old age sense of the sacrifice, where the person is simply absorbed into an abstraction called the whole, or the state, or the group. One ceases to be a dynamic creative, self-fulfilled participant.

In custodianship, in true sacrifice, in true synthesis, there is no loss of identity but rather the realisation of a greater identity. It is from the perspective of that greater identity that activities are generated, action is taken, and the energies come forward to create the group consciousness.

The politics of such a group revolve around evolution, around service, around custodianship, around mutual empowerment, not around domination, manipulation, and control. The politics of synergy are the politics of goodwill, of service, of a will to understand, a will to love, an illuminated intelligence, and wisdom.

To me this represents the course of our future. These are the politics that will evolve in the Aquarian Age. What form it takes on national levels and international levels has yet to be seen. Perhaps it will take the form of a large number of service organisations arising, and even nations themselves conceiving of themselves as being organs of service and of light and of synergy within the greater planetary whole.

Certainly the politics of synergy will reinterpret humanity's relationship to nature, to the use of natural resources, its relationships with animals and plants, and to everything that makes up the environment. When we consider that the bulk of politics today is based on fear, aggression and defensiveness, all of which are based on concepts of separation, we can see that in a state of mind and consciousness, and in a group and in a group of groups where the awareness of separation is dispelled and an awareness of oneness, of unity and of dynamic cooperation and goodwill is substituted, the whole spectrum of international and national politics as we know it must disappear and be transformed into something quite unrecognisable by today's standards.

How can we bring this about? By allowing custodianship, sacrifice, and synthesis to begin with oneself.

How do you stand in relationship to your world, to the things you own, to your family, to your job and employees, or to your employer?

85

How able are you to sacrifice truly, not with a martyr complex, not with a sense of giving up, but with a sense of taking on and moving in consciousness to a greater identity?

How able are you to be a custodian within your life?

How able are you to create states of synergy with the people with whom you must relate and work?

Can you be an agent in your community to form groups that can explore the dynamics of group development, of the politics of synergy? Can you reduce the elements of fear, of separation, of prejudice, of nationalism in your life, and substitute for them greater understanding of other people and cultures, a lack of fear, a courage, a love, a wisdom?

If you can, and if you do these things, then you are helping to build the new world. You are a politician of synergy.

Let us each be a politician of synergy. No one need elect us. Support need not come from a majority. It comes from the divinity that we are, which we in turn can use to recognise the one divinity that is within all things. Through the recognition of oneness and brotherhood as an actual fact of evolution—not as an ideal, not as a possible Utopian social state but as an actual fact, just as sunlight is a fact and chlorophyll is a fact—we are in a position to translate that fact into reality, and to build a new world, a world governed and a world growing through the politics of synergy.

Chapter Nine
MY WORLD VIEW:
A PERSONAL VISION

A CENTRE like Findhorn exists because a planetary birth is taking place, and men and women of many cultures are now in the process of becoming the instruments through which this birth can take place. Things are also happening in the realms of nature with the devas, the elementals, and probably in kingdoms that we are unaware of; but we are human beings, and we tend to interpret things from the perspective of the human kingdom. Therefore the birth of a new world, the birth of a new age, is probably best considered as an action taking place within human consciousness. If changes are not made in human consciousness, the rest of the world and all other kingdoms can undergo transformation and we will fail to recognise it, so we will fail to enter a new world. Actually, we might find ourselves not part of any world in that case.

So what we are asked to engage in is psychological change. The birth of a new planet is basically the personal birth of a new individuality. The birth of a new world is the birth of a new image of humanity, collectively and individually; and Findhorn, like many individuals and centres also striving to embody this planetary action, is a womb within which this birth can occur.

What are some of the characteristics of this birth from my perspective? We begin with humanity. Humanity as I see it stands at a crossover point in evolution. It is straddling two dimensions of life. Humanity is part of the natural environment, the ecological environment, part of those worlds which we call the worlds of form and matter. Its roots reach back into the organic and inorganic history of the planet.

Then there is an aspect of humanity which could be called extraterrestrial. Not that it comes here in any kind of space-craft, but only that it is not a product of Earth's evolution. It is a product of an evolutionary process which is beyond this planet. It is cosmic. In a sense, that aspect of humanity has been invoked by the Earth aspect. When a certain point of dynamic tension was reached in evolutionary history, this invocation took place. The ancient texts say that the Lords of Flame descended upon the Earth, kindled the spark of embryonic individuation, and the flame of mind began to burn.

There is also a third aspect of humanity, and to me this is a key aspect: the divine self. It is an aspect of humanity through which it relates in oneness to all other aspects of the universe. At that level man and deva are one, man and elemental are one, man and the stars are one, and we are one with kingdoms of life of which we have no present knowledge.

This source identity is what is seeking birth or greater externalisation through form, because it alone has the capacity to resolve the many dichotomies and paradoxes that are born in the realm of form, like good and evil, light and dark, male and female, spirit and matter.

When humanity emerged from this source consciousness, it required the creation of a state of dynamic tension which could produce energy. This state was created through this intermeshing of a highly organised, highly evolved and highly intelligent material self, or Earth self, and a highly ephemeral, highly refined, almost star-like high energy self which we could call the spirit, the spiritual self.

When these two come together, they are different from each other, so they must work at·relating; they must work at blending. Out of that work something is generated—a new form of life, a new body. A vehicle is created which is the synergetic blending of spirit and matter, in such a way that that vehicle is neither spirit nor matter. Do not try to think of it in terms of a body like a physical body. It can function through a physical body. A person can be in a physical body and yet psychologically, psychically, spiritually, be functioning through this transcendental form.

This transcendental form is the true form of humanity. It has only rarely been expressed in comparison to the great numbers of human beings that exist in relationship to this world, both in incarnation and out of it. Those that have achieved it and are functioning through that synthesis, we call the Masters or the Hierarchy. They are best understood as being true representatives of the human race. The majority of humanity is still in the chrysalis stage, still in the stage of undergoing those internal transformations within the cocoon of self and self-awareness that will eventually allow that meshing and that new form to come about.

Therefore I view a person as a being in which two states of polarity are striving to come together within the magnetic field of self-

88

hood; a dynamic tension among three points of a triangle: self-awareness, the physical-earth-elemental entity, and the spiritual entity. Out of that fusion, that creative blending, humanity's divine identity is revealed.

Before continuing, I need to say something about this divine identity, about God. Interestingly enough, people quite often define themselves in relationship to a divine image. How people see themselves is often a function of how they define God. It might be said that when this energy of life emerged, and humanity began the quest to manifest this transcendental form, it invoked from itself an 'I—Thou' relationship; and part of itself then became an overlighting divine power capable of generating the experience and the forms and the life energy which this embryonic humanity, this divine spark, could use to build up whatever it would require to accomplish its ends. It moved through a pattern requiring structure and form, and God took the image of the creative source, the image of the parent, the loving guide.

Of course, when we are trying to trace the history of the divine idea we could go back further than that, but I want to use that as my starting point. What is inherent within people and within this external God-form, created when people necessarily moved into the experience of selfhood (which is a state of separation from the rest of the cosmos) was the potential of a relationship which would inevitably draw these two together. Once the individual learns that she or he is the possessor of divinity and not simply the creation of divinity, then that relationship begins to come into focus.

I have sought to express that relationship through using a term like the Beloved. Part of that is born from my own experience of an energy on a higher level which is very, very loving. It is not loving in those particularly exclusive ways in which we are normally accustomed to thinking of love in our personality world, unless you can imagine an extremely impersonal and yet very intimate kind of love.

Through the use of the term 'Beloved' I have sought to convey an idea that humanity has the potential of entering into a one-to-one relationship with that essence that we have called God, a relationship that is intensely and supremely creative: not humanity reaching to a greater form but humanity recognising a divine polarity which reaches out for its mate.

The symbolism of this may be found in the man or the woman who leaves the household of the parents, unites with a beloved and

89

then begins to create his or her own household. When a person is in one's parents' house it is the parents who hold ultimate authority, because they are ultimately responsible for what takes place in that household. But when the children become the adults and are on their own, they have the responsibility.

This concept of the term 'Beloved', to me, conveys not just a nice, cosy, warm relationship with God, but rather the realisation that life is placing upon myself a very intimate and very intense and very real responsibility: not the sagging shoulders, weight-of-the world, bow-your-head kind of responsibility, but one that is joyous and uplifting and exhilarating because it is a recognition of what I am. It is an opportunity to make at least a small step towards affirming my role, my creative role, in the world process.

If I define God as a presence of supreme life and creative intelligence, a source with which I may merge to also express source-like qualities, then my image of myself must undergo alteration. I cannot be simply a tool or an instrument in the hands of a being separate from myself. I cannot be humble in the sense of seeing myself in an unrealistic perspective which casts me into a position where I am simply the recipient of life energies and where things happen to me because of forces outside my control.

True humility, to my way of thinking, is the sense of a vision that enables me to see my responsibility to an evolving wholeness and to recognise that I am a facet of a great organism, a great being. At the same time I *am* that being, not a fragment of it. I am the wholeness of the being, expressing in a very particular way, and if that wholeness is to be affirmed and realised than I also must affirm your position in that being and see you in a realistic perspective, in a perspective of oneness.

The divinity within is the most difficult thing for people to come to grips with. We want to be divine, we want God-realisation, but our tendency is to play games with it, to perceive it in terms of phenomena or in terms of becoming imbued with miraculous powers.

There is something very commonplace about divinity that I think gets overlooked except in places like Findhorn. This is one of its strengths. Somewhere in this world, after all, there is a divinity that is working away at rocks with the tools of wind and waves, and there is a divinity that grows little blades of grass and tiny flowers that hide behind larger flowers; there is a divinity that makes mountains, and there is a divinity that encompasses oceans; there is a divinity that does everything that needs to be done to express itself, no matter how large or how minute. And it does it with a sense of, "If I am an ocean I have to be an ocean; if I am a pond I have to be a pond. I am what I need to be in this place, in this time, so that the whole can be made manifest."

Divinity is a sense of "I love the place where I am at and the contribution I can make to the whole." Divinity is a sense of that awareness which strives for excellence in what it does. If I am cleaning the floor, that is as divine, as God-involved, as being in meditation or speaking to a hundred thousand people at the Houston Astrodome.

Divinity is commonplace. Seen that way, however, the commonplace becomes miraculous and spectacular.

Divinity—this third element, this impulse toward transcendency—demands that it will express itself. It demands that in some fashion spirit and matter will come together to give it birth. Its objectives do not embrace keeping spirit and matter comfortable. Its objectives embrace drawing out of spirit and matter that which will dissolve them as separate polarities and express them as a synthesised wholeness.

Therefore in some ways divinity means death as well as birth. It means courage to grow, courage to expand, to change, to be open to the forces within one that would lead out and transcend different stages of self-awareness. Yet paradoxically divinity is also that which will seek to perfect the stages of self, for it is through that balance and excellence of manifestation that this synthesis can best be achieved.

In many cases we seek after images of divinity, the symbols of divinity rather than the reality. We seek after that which we are not and forget that divinity is what we are—not necessarily as a form and yet as a form; not in our present psychological make-up and yet in some way behind that psychological make-up. At this time of history, an energy and a world that manifests that energy are seeking externalisation, and they will represent a world in which this third aspect, or this transcendency aspect, or this wholeness aspect can be more clearly discerned. This world is emerging not in opposition to the world that we presently experience; it is emerging not as a new age following an old age; it is emerging as something that has been behind all the ages, and it is not going to emerge totally in the next two thousand years. It is a long-term project.

A very significant change in human consciousness is occurring now, one which I have called Birth Three, a change as important and as significant as that when humanity first gained the power to think. Humanity is now gaining the power to do something for which we have no name: perhaps to think beyond thought, to be beyond being, to will beyond will. Humanity as the beloved of the Earth, humanity as the collective consciousness and therefore as the individual consciousness, has the capacity to transform the Earth because the Earth is like the branch of a tree or a plant on which the caterpillar spins its cocoon and the butterfly emerges, and the butterfly in turn has the capacity to pollinate that flower of that plant and enable it to fulfil its destiny.

The Earth has no future except through humanity's capacity to be the instrument for its transformation. Humanity must resolve through its own consciousness this ancient dichotomy of spirit and matter, God and creation, all the dualities, all the perceptions that we have worked with for so very long. From a point of creative identification, of knowing its divine reality and identity and perspective, humanity will then be able to reach out and embrace the Earth and all the other kingdoms of life from the source from which they have come and enable them to take their next step.

Humanity must be transformed to make this possible. A group of individuals is required upon the Earth not as an organisation, not as anything that could really be defined in human institutional terms, but as a living organism composed of individuals who know their place, their perspective, their identity as part of a human whole and a planetary whole—who know that just as I could take a cell from my body and through a process known as cloning re-create my body—since the cells of my body contain the essential genetic code from which the entire body is constructed—so each of us as a human being contains the entire genetic code from which this planet has been born and from which humanity has been born. It is theoretically possible through a kind of spiritual science to pluck any person out of this room and recreate the Earth and humanity on all its levels. But all of us together, by experiencing the essence of the wholeness, by seeing ourselves as agents of this planetary whole—which in no way makes us self-less but indeed makes us supremely more than we could ever be in an isolated position—by taking that consciousness in, we become a contributing, co-creative part of this evolving humanhood.

Several times in my life I have had a very clear vision, not so much in form but in essence. It began when I was seven years old, although at that time I did not really know what it was, had no way of relating it to anything. This was a vision of a sphere of life enveloping the Earth, merging into the Earth like a giant inbreath and then emerging out again, and out of this re-emergence, this outbreath, the Earth becoming transformed. That process of transformation is like watching a body take shape: a centre here and an individual there, becoming strong, embodying a new pattern as best it can, and then reaching out to link with a centre over there, or a person over there, propagating itself until a momentum is built up, a tremendous energy field established, a chain reaction, with people beginning to recognise that while change occurred in the past through external action—the necessity to move people along because they did not have the awareness or the capacity to move themselves—they now possess the capacity to recognise a creative responsibility in their roles. With hands of flesh and hands of time humanity is beginning to grasp the energies of time and of space, of psyche and of being, and to say, "I will that these energies will now reflect the divinity that is within all things; I will that this energy that forms my world as it passes through me will become the flesh, the substance, the breath of a new world, and that in so doing I learn to perceive divinity as a participatory process of creative service, creative self-transcendence, creative awareness, creative life and light and love and wisdom and communion with all others who can join me on that level, link with me in that way and also become builders of the Earth, seed points from which this new is emerging."

And it will emerge. It will emerge very quickly, as a matter of fact, in terms of human history. The crux of this evolutionary change through which humanity is moving will have passed within the next fifty to seventy-five years. In a sense the balance has already been tipped. We shall achieve this shift. The birth has already occurred, and it is now simply a process of divine embryology.

My vision is this vision of each of us being asked to make a supreme leap in imagination and in consciousness; to recognise not an image of God or an image of humanity, but the synthesis of the two of them; to be aware that a new Christhood is coming into being.

Christ is a term that means the anointed one. What is emerging as the Christ of our time embraces that concept, just as the Christ

Jesus embraced the prophetic traditions and the avatar traditions that preceded him. It will not be so much humanity being anointed by God, as humanity learning the magical process of giving birth to God and allowing divinity to participate in the continuity of evolution and of growth and of the excitement of creativity, which, after all, is divinity's second nature. This image is of humanity as the children of God and yet in a subtle way the progenitors of God, and in all ways one with the divine, now being asked to take responsibility, disciplined responsibility, for the energies with which people identify themselves, for the energies that they extend into the world. They are asked to learn the magic, the wonder and the ritual of communion, how to work in group consciousness, how to be a point of focus through which a wholeness can manifest, both within a particular part and in a whole, in a group.

This particular vision is also Findhorn's vision. That is what those of Findhorn are participating in. This makes the work at Findhorn important, because this vision of humanity is subtle and in some ways involves energies for which we have no terminology as yet. But it can be lived and demonstrated. It can actually be invoked because it is present already, around us, within us: but it takes a group to do it. It takes individuals with awareness and with love to do it.

In a group where people come from different paths, words have been used to mean different things. For example, some come through a path which teaches the overcoming of the personality and its becoming infused by the light of the soul. On the other hand, I come from a path in which, as a human-relations counsellor, my whole work was to help people function in their personalities more effectively. Reaching for the soul without having a balanced personality would mean not having a proper foundation to encompass that greater energy.

In one sense the personality is simply an image that other people see. It is the way we reflect the world—and to that extent we will always have a personality. A being in a physical form, attuned to the highest energy that this planet could withstand, could walk into this room and we would each see him as having a personality. We would probably each see him as having a slightly different personality. For those who are interested, the marvellous book by Kahlil Gibran, *Jesus the Son of Man*, which portrays Jesus as seen through the eyes of about fifty different people, is an illustration of this. In a sense, however, what we would be seeing is a reflection of ourselves from the mirror of that being's consciousness. So what we would say is that that being's personality is really a reflection of our personality. To that extent, I am sure we have all experienced the phenomenon in which we see in others the things we most dislike in ourselves—the things that are most apparent in ourselves. Not always, of course, but that is a factor of what we see. On that level, no matter how spiritual you become, you always have a personality in the eyes of other people. So there is that definition of personality.

The next level is the actual mechanism of self-relatedness to the environment, the relationship to the environment which we have formed over the process of time, which acts like a cocoon within which deeper energies are being merged and fused and metamorphosed into a new life. The whole process of this phase of human evolution could be described· as individualisation and the development of selfhood and self-awareness. That requires a personality, and occultly what is meant in this case by a personality is the combined energies of the physical, the etheric, the astral or feeling body and the mental body—the gestalt of these four plus the specific manifestations of each of them as four separate energy bodies. Those four separately and together make up what is called the personality from an occult sense. That is a vehicle or combination of them.

The personality can reflect the divine or it can obscure it by manifesting divine fragments. We are trying to manifest a oneness through a multiplicity of levels all at once. This is a process in which these levels interact and split up the divine light like a prism, and reflect back its certain instrinsic qualities which we experience in a myriad ways, from the spectrum of extreme pleasure to extreme pain. All this interaction makes up the personality.

Each of these levels feeds itself. It draws energy from its own level: emotions feed on emotions, the mind feeds on thought, and the body feeds on physical substance. This process of living interaction with the environment on all these levels creates the personality, but all of this can obstruct manifestion of that essential wholeness.

The process of shedding the personality is a process of ceasing to function as the tool of a fragment of consciousness. I am no longer motivated by an emotional outburst, or by a thought alone, or by a physical need. I am able to get it together within myself, in a sense to fuse these so fully and dynamically that they become a single vessel. They become what symbolically is called the Holy Grail, because as soon as that infused personality is created the communion is experienced with a higher level and that communion fills and transforms the personality.

The personality is, as we use the term, that which limits us. I suppose we shall always need a term for that which is our tester, and 'personality' is as good a name as any. But we need to be careful that we are precise in what we mean, because functioning on a personality level is only an obstruction when the personality is uncoordinated and in essence acting in different directions within itself; and as it is unable to blend with others, it fragments.

In this sense the personality has a mission—the mission of drawing things in. In essence the personality is nothing more than a womb; it has as its mission pulling things into a centre and intensifying them. In another metaphor, it is like a greenhouse. It is that which focuses experience to such an intense kind of self-involvement the being cannot stand it any more until with an understanding of selfhood it bursts forth and can understand the meaning of the divine self.

The personality looks inward. Its basic motion is inbreath. The motion of the soul is outbreath. The keynote of the personality is to take. The keynote of the soul is to give. When the personality becomes more and more attuned to the soul, it alters its desire to take and begins to allow the outbreath to emerge. It is when the personality is still acting in its womb state, pulling in, beyond the time when it should act that way for that particular being, that it becomes an obstruction. In a centre like Findhorn it can be an obstruction, because the task here is to infuse the personality with creative energy and to use it as a tool, not to allow it to be the point of identity which determines the way in which energy is expressed or the way in which we relate.

What will be a symbol of that initiation whereby the personality ceases to exist as a separate vehicle and symbolically the butterfly emerges from the chrysalis which that personality represented? I cannot answer that in terms of what the initiation will change into, because if it has been determined, it has not been externalised yet to the best of my knowledge. I am not at all sure that it can be externalised except through a group. In some fashion I know it is group-involved. We are moving into an age of group initiation as opposed to individual initiation.

It will probably take the form of a level of intensive group work, by means of which each person in the ritual of group life, in the dynamics of group life, creates a point of energy within which the personality dissolves and a greater energy emerges—a love energy, a wisdom energy.

Every expansion of consciousness which is an initiation is essentially motivated by an increase in the love capacity of the being, on one level or another, and the ability of that love to manifest in different ways, as light, as wisdom and so on. At this stage and in this cycle of evolution, love is the great initiator. Externally Jesus was crucified but subjectively he sacrificed himself, or he expanded himself into a greater identity through love. That of course is why the crucifixion was such an important symbol in the past, because esoterically it represents not so much the shattering of the personality but the giving up of a specific focus in order that a love might move out into identification with humanity, and therefore uplift humanity in very important ways.

I say that crucifixion will cease to be an initiatory symbol because the symbol has now obscured the reality. It has become an emotionally charged, devotionally charged symbol by which people invoke crucifixion to themselves without exploring other ways in which the same process of transformation could conceivably take place. The process will remain but the way in which we perceive it may need to change.

Chapter Ten
THE EVOLUTION OF GOVERNMENT

HUMANITY is really the great imitator on earth. Many human inventions and developments are derived directly from nature. Sonar, for instance, comes from both marine animals like the dolphin and the porpoise, and from mammals like the bat. The whole development of aircraft was inspired by the structure of birds. Many of the ways in which people have done things have been preceded by natural phenomena. In Freemasonry, in which an individual is trained to perceive and fulfil his divine role of being a mason or a builder in creation, God is seen as the great architect of the universe and all human forms are in turn seen as being derived from divine forms which can be seen in the world.

This is also true in the way humanity establishes its social structures. Government did not originate with humanity; it originated with beings who were the original teachers of humanity. It was a very long time ago, but people at one time possessed the natural capacity of what we would call clairvoyance, and were fully attuned to the mind and will of nature. This attunement was guided and directed by beings who acted as teachers, those beings, primarily from other streams of evolution more advanced than the human, who cultivated within people the qualities of awareness they needed to have.

In doing so they served as points of focus to clarify an awareness of natural structure and law, an awareness which people already possessed to a significant degree because they were for all practical purposes still part of the group soul of nature. We may today, with the interest in psychic phenomena and the premium that is placed upon people who are sensitive, look upon that ancient time as being a glorious time when people could walk and talk with beings of great light, when they could see the devas and the angels and the elementals, when they could hear the voice of nature speaking to them in its many parts: in wind, in the sound of water and the roll of thunder. What we have now, however, and what we are going to have in the course of our development, is far greater than that which early people possessed, for all their sensitivity.

I have heard the voice of nature, perhaps as early people may have heard it, though I do not think to the same intensity, and it is quite an awesome experience. To be frank, I am very glad I do not have to listen to it very often, because nature speaks with an overwhelming quality of 'groupness' in which the quality of the individual is completely overwhelmed. You are simply a part of a universal flow and cannot be anything else.

Humanity is at a point in its evolution where it has left that instinctive group attunement behind. It has been divinely closed off, because unless this were so people could not develop the inner qualities of Godhood which they possess.

Nevertheless, humanity is rooted in nature, and when I say it is good that we do not hear the voice of nature, I do not mean by that that it is good that we are apart from nature or even that we ignore the rhythms and harmonies of the natural world. We ignore them at our own risk.

We are rooted in natural processes. The force that is behind the natural world is the same force that is within us, and if we hear a voice speaking very loudly in our environment, the chances are we will not hear the much subtler and quieter voice that speaks within our own hearts and being. It is the same voice, but this shift of focus is quite important, and before we can graduate from the experiences which Earth has to offer we have to learn to recognise and become at one with the inner voice. There will come a time when we will be asked to step free of Earth into the immensities of cosmic experience, and the voice of nature as we know it will no longer be present. It will be superseded by a much greater power and rhythm, and if we have not learned that inner strength we will be unable to function in the presence of such power.

There are hints of this in the ancient mysteries and in the writings of prophets of various religions, particularly within our Judeo-Christian heritage, where the Holy of Holies was not open to the average individuals. The High Priest in Jerusalem only entered the most sacred point of the temple once a year. It was said then that to see the face of God was to be destroyed. To touch the Ark of the Covenant was to court death. Occultly, this is true, and it is also true psychologically.

Before humanity can stand before God and receive the accolades which are its right and the diploma that is its heritage, it must have recognised that presence in itself. We must see the whole course of human history as arising out of the womb of nature into a greater awareness of the microcosmic reflections of that womb within our own being, and into the ability to become at one with that which is within us and to bring it to the fore.

Humanity recognises that these laws with which it is working are the same laws that govern all of creation. Whatever humanity's attunement to nature, however deeply it has been enmeshed in nature's group consciousness and however humanity tries to move free of it into the awareness of its own individual divinity, the teachers of the race have always asked humanity to use nature as a text book and to be able to perceive reflected there the operation of laws which are universal.

The original government which humanity experienced was by our terms not a government at all. It was much more compulsory than any government that we are aware of, for human will was not developed to the point where people had a concept of self identity. They simply obeyed in the same way that the elementals obey. They were part of a rhythm, and it was inconceivable that they could do anything that was in opposition to that rhythm.

Those who could be called in our terminology governors were individuals who could interpret this rhythm for people. Since embryonic humanity was not capable of grasping the immensity of the rhythms of nature on all levels, these rhythms had to be interpreted within the scope of existing awareness. For example, if certain tasks needed to be done, there had to be someone to point this out and to show how these tasks fitted in with the rhythm of whatever natural processes were involved. People did these tasks quite uncomplainingly and learned in doing them.

As people developed and became more aware of themselves as separate beings, they still recognised the power and the necessity or importance of these non-human or superhuman beings who were their instructors.

The relationship was not so much that between ruler and subjects as that between teacher and pupils. That has always been the relationship between the advanced members of the race and the rest of humanity. The concept of a spiritual elite ruling the world is one of humanity's dreams, but it is not a reality. The concept of spiritual educators uplifting the world is the reality.

There is a subtle difference here. It is an important difference to hold in mind because a number of very pure spiritual teachings, a number of great brotherhoods including the Rosicrucian, have

100

often been perverted through the ages by the action of their members to establish themselves as a spiritual and philosophical elite, capable of ruling in the name of God but actually ruling because they conceive themselves to be an elite.

The early teachers of the race pointed out that nature is a hierarchy. Nature is a tyranny really, a benevolent one but tyrannical nonetheless, because there is no escape from the laws of nature. One cannot decide that one will rebel against the law of gravity. One obeys it and asks no questions.

This is true with all natural law, the laws that govern our life. When we seek to disobey them we die, because we ourselves are the outgrowth of these laws. These laws are not so much laws but manifestations of the very structure and rhythm that is the essence of our own being.

In the early tribal societies, rulership went to the individual who proved most capable of fulfilling the needs of the tribe. If those needs involved hunting, it was the most skilled hunter, the strongest, the bravest, the one who most understood the ways of the animals they were stalking. If it was an agricultural community, perhaps the leader was the one who seemed best able to fulfil the needs of the community in making the crops grow. This might be a priest, for example, someone who was 'in' with the weather gods and the gods of fertility and soil.

In ancient Greece an attempt was made to establish a pure democracy, but a democracy in which the individuals who ruled the community were the most advanced intellectually and artistically. As Athenian history shows, however, this very rarely worked out in practice because of various elements of human corruption and self-seeking on the part of the people who took over offices of responsibility.

The great empires of the past such as Egypt and the empires of the East were ruled over by individuals who were priest-kings. These all had to be high initiates. They had to have gone through the experience of the second birth, which means that they could function as freely on the inner realms as they could on the physical realms. In essence, they were the embodiment of the soul of the people.

It was realised in those days that a true ruler was not one who made law; that nobody had the right to make a law; all that the ruler could do was to interpret the divine laws which already were in existence, according to the needs of the people. Therefore the

101

ancient rulers were all put through initiatory rites to free their consciousness from their bodies, to open within them cosmic awareness so that they had clear and direct knowledge of what the divine laws were, as well as the wisdom to interpret them for their people.

These individuals were absolute rulers in the same sense that nature is an absolute ruler. They ceased to be human beings in the way that we now think of a human being, but became embodiments of a spiritual presence. They were a spiritual presence, in fact.

Of course, when the priesthood became corrupt in Egypt, the throne became weak and equally corrupt. The gift of rulership was perverted into a form of tyranny without wisdom, tyranny without the cosmic power that gives the right to be an absolute ruler.

The same thing was true with the early kings. The concept of kingship is really a spiritual one and again it is based on what we see in nature. It is the rule of the individual who is the most capable within a given society, who has literally the broadest vision, the greatest consciousness—the individual who is closest to the embodiment of the whole society. The early kings were just such individuals. On whatever level their consciousness could function, they represented the embodiment of the good of the society. But when humanity began to lose its contact with spirit, as humanity's inherent sensitivities began to be turned off in order to learn to listen to the voice within, kingship became perverted.

Once I saw an interesting film concerning the life of Napoleon. Napoleon was an individual who was sent with a divine destiny to create in Europe something equivalent to the United States of America. His task was to lay a foundation for a United Europe, with one set of laws, one basic language, one coinage, and to eliminate the kind of strife that we have had for the past two hundred years in Europe.

Unfortunately, as Napoleon gained the power to do this, when he moved into the position where he was able to accomplish this, it went to his head. This was symbolically evident when it was time for him to be crowned Emperor and he seized the crown from the bishop and placed it on his own head. This is very symbolic of an individual's saying, "It is I who am crowning myself. It is not God." It was at this point that the spiritual powers of the world that had been backing him and had been responsible for many of his successes withdrew. It was at that point that Napoleon began to go downhill.

Why is nature, the structure of the Earth, the way it is? It is because nature has the task of taking energy from a very pure and cosmic state and adapting it to several levels of expression. Many of these levels have no capacity whatsoever either to attune to or withstand the full impact of pure energy or cosmic energy any more than one would try to put too much electricity through a simple circuit. The fuse would blow.

Therefore the energy flows through graded steps, and it is these steps and their personification that we call the hierarchy. This really must be understood: that the hierarchy is not a governing body, it is an educative body on the one hand and it is a natural force on the other, designed to step down energy so that it is universally available.

You have the same process in your body. There is only one point, normally speaking, in which food in its normal state can enter your body, and that is through your mouth. That food, even though you have eaten it and swallowed it, is still outside your body. It is surrounded by your body, but until it is digested it is unavailable as an energy source to any of your cells. You could put your hand next to a carrot or a piece of chocolate cake, but if you did nothing else your hand would eventually wither from starvation, because the cells of your hand have no ability to assimilate food directly through osmosis. You have become so specialised that other organs are required to put the food through a long digestive process to break it down into its component parts and carry that nourishment to the cells.

People are somewhat in that position, but nature—the natural world, the minerals, the vegetables, the animals—are very much in that condition. They are unable to draw nourishment directly from a cosmic source, and so the hierarchy on its many levels breaks it down and makes it available on a level that such forms can assimilate.

The point of entry for this energy is through a being who is known as the Lord of the World. This being is also the king or the head of the hierarchy, and the energy proceeds from there to the various positions of consciousness which represent the heads of seven 'rays', or creative attributes. From there it goes to still further departments, until eventually it is available to evolving consciousness. It is this vision that inspired human forms of government for a long time, for many centuries, and which gave birth to the concept of the absolute ruler, the individual who was the point of focus through which divine inspiration would come and be mediated to the people.

As humanity has progressed, however, two things have happened. The first thing is that the awareness of natural law has diminished. Awareness of internal personal law has increased, which is another way of saying that humanity has become more self-oriented through the past few centuries, more aware of being separate and less aware of being part of nature. With the development and enhancement of mind through the industrial revolutions over the past two hundred years, this condition has been accelerated and has increased, so that in modern days we have a situation where in the Western world the majority of people are out of touch with natural rhythms, and instead are coming into tune with purely artificial rhythms existing in our urban centres and in our civilisation.

This close down was brought about through removing natural clairvoyance and the awareness of the inner realms of nature and life. Humanity was left alone to grow because it could grow in no other way. It had to be weaned from the Earth.

In practical terms the result of this has been the creation of a state of anarchy upon the Earth. As people seek to discover new laws of rhythm and to free themselves from the old laws, they are going through a very lengthy interim period which has nothing to do with Piscean or Aquarian ages. It is an interim period of consciousness in which they are in that middle point of being a law unto themselves. Each individual is a law unto oneself, and this creates a form of chaos.

Of recent years human society has been devised to try and keep order in the midst of this chaos, and as a consequence the concept of government has changed subtly from being one of management and good organisation to see that materials flow properly, and government for educational purposes, to government for the purpose of providing structure and order, government for the purpose of creating law and discipline.

In other words, the relationship between the ruler and the subjects has become less that of teacher and pupil and more that of ruler and subject. Much of this has been necessary, of course. Much of it is motivated by fear. It is an attempt to keep attuned to the rhythms of structure and law so that in this period of growth people can maintain their direction and not lose it.

This period of growth is one in which each individual is asked to learn to govern oneself, to become responsible in the keenest sense possible. The highest form of individual government is self-government, not government by one individual with the support and the consent of the many.

Because of this need for people to learn self-government, however, there has arisen the next great step, democracy. Democracy is one of the major evolutionary steps. The concept originated with the Greeks, who practised it. The Swiss still have a much purer form of democracy than any other large state on earth. America and Britain seek to practice democracy but it is more appropriately a form of republicanism, because the people do not make policy decisions directly. They elect representatives who guide the country.

The essence of democracy is a state resting upon a group of individuals who are aware of themselves as divine beings and are attuned to the good of the whole. Democracy cannot function under any other conditions. Until it reaches that condition, democracy is the attempt of the personality to work its will with the support of other people. If I want to do something and can get the majority behind me, I am supported in what I wish to do, whether it is right or not.

Democracy is a great experiment on the part of the spiritual forces, and a vitally necessary one. It is also a risk, because of all forms of government it is the one most open to chaos and anarchy.

A totalitarian state definitely has its advantages, but it is not evolutionary any more. Rulership by one individual has its advantages but it is retrogressive. Humanity needs to have demonstrated a form of attunement and consciousness which can set the pattern not so much for new forms of government but for bringing the forms of government that already exist back into attunement.

Democracy in America is increasingly falling apart, and the original freedoms that Americans had are reduced. They are not the same as they were two hundred years ago. Democracy is falling apart simply because of excessive self-interest. This is true in Britain, too. Yet the society of consciousness of the future—not necessarily the immediate future, but what humanity is moving toward—is a democratic society in the sense that it is the whole that rules.

The whole is not the sum of the individual parts. The whole is the spirit that embraces and moves through all the parts and yet is greater than any one of them, greater even than the totality of them. We then come full circle, because the original initiate kings were only representatives of the whole. They were by no means single rulers in the sense that we know them today, like certain sheikhs in the Middle East. The ancient priest-kings were not absolute rulers in that sense. They were representatives of the spirit of the whole and embodied democracy on the lower level of the spiral, except that the spirit that guided them was not the conscious voice of their people but its unconscious voice—its hopes, dreams, yearnings, and its desires for the future.

The great evolutionary experiment in which humanity is involved is: How can humanity find its conscious articulation of the divine spirit, and through that articulation, through that wisdom, select those leaders who will most represent that spirit? And then how can it follow the inspiration and direction which these leaders give, because the function of a leader is to provide just that little bit of extra vision which the rest do not have, to be just that little bit more attuned to the dreams and hopes and future of the community or the country or the race of which they are the representatives?

All spiritual societies are hierarchical. They cannot function in any other way. That has been an ironclad rule in the past, simply because spiritual societies derive themselves from individuals who are points of focus for the spirit, from those who are most attuned down to those who are least attuned because they are the newest, the neophytes, the probationers, those who are just entering into awareness.

It is obvious that in conducting the affairs of a spiritual society one would not turn to those who are least attuned. One turns to those who are most attuned. That is what a spiritual society is all about. It is not the will of the majority that is important. It is the will of the whole, the spirit of the whole, and the whole is not the majority; the whole is that manifestation of Christ life, of spiritual life moving within each whether they are aware of it or not, which can only function for the good of each and maintain the wholeness of each. It is not quantitative. Democracy as we know it is a quantitative form of government. True democracy, however, is qualitative, and that is what we must return to.

At Findhorn we have a particular challenge—and I think this will be true of most new age groups who seek to pioneer the vision of a new society—because we are a spiritual society. We are being governed by individuals whose vision we trust as being highly attuned to the good of the whole, and these individuals are the leaders of the community. No one here has elected these leaders. Findhorn does not work on the basis of such an election.

On the other hand the evolutionary impulse is a democratic one, which means that each individual comes to the point where one is self-governing through one's attunement, and able through that attunement to be a representative of the whole.

It requires a considerable balance and experimentation to create a 'theocratic democracy'; which is a fascinating concept, suggesting what we are moving towards for humankind.

Words are a problem here because human hierarchies are entirely different from spiritual ones. A human hierarchy is composed of individuals; the spiritual hierarchy is one whole. We see many masters in it representing different levels, but to a person who is consciously part of the hierarchy there is only one being, one spirit, one will, one consciousness, one awareness. It is not made up of a number of people. In other words, the hierarchy is a purely human concept. It has no meaning once you step outside of a human point of reference, because through our conditioning over the past few hundred years we are now thinking in terms of law, of rulership, of discipline, of how to maintain order through what could be called the dark night of the soul for the race, the period of greatest potential chaos. But at some point we have to go beyond that consciousness if the race is to achieve the destiny that is its heritage. It cannot be done by democracy alone, nor by monarchy alone, nor by any humanly conceived governmental structure. It can only be done through attunement and revelation on all levels.

In nature that which has the greatest capacity has the greatest authority. It is really a very simple principle. I would not attempt to fix my car because I know nothing about mechanics. I would get someone who is skilled in that, and if they told me I needed to do a certain thing I would do it, because I recognise their competence in an area where I am not competent. On the other hand, if someone came to me with a problem relating to an occult or spiritual thing, I would expect that same deference or giving over of authority to me in that field, because that is where I am competent. It is simply a matter of where we are skilled and trained to function. That is a natural pattern, and if it establishes a hierarchy then that is the way human beings look at it. What it really establishes is a wholeness, a wholeness that is created continually by each of its parts, fulfilling its appropriate function at that time.

When an individual has attunement and responsibility in an area and has been told "It is your task now to attune to a higher pattern and bring it into focus and manifest it," then that individual has to be given complete authority. If the success or non-success of the venture rests upon him, if he has the responsibility, he should have the authority, and those who are working with him need to acquiesce to that. If there is any problem, then the democratic solution is not to put that person in a postion of authority next time.

The challenge at Findhorn is to find an expression of consciousness which will mark the next evolutionary step, which will give it a chance to express. It has to be compounded of the best of democracy and the best of the old pattern which recognises the right of rulership of those who are the most capable and the most attuned in a given situation. More than that, it must recognise that what we are attempting to move out of is a state in which government is for governing. What we seek to move toward is a state where government is for management and the proper use of resources on the one hand, and for education on the other; for the proper release of the resources of consciousness of the people who are under the charge of the governor.